The Christina:

The Onassis Odyssey

Celebrities, Courtships & Chaos

compiled and written

by

January Jones

P. J. Publishing

The Christina: The Onassis Odyssey Celebrities, Courtships & Chaos

January Jones

Published by:
    P. J. Publishing
    info@januaryjones.com
    www.januaryjones.com

Cover Photo: AP/World Wide Photos

Copyright 2007 by January Jones
Printed in the United States of America

Original Cover Design by Sierra Crook

ISBN-13: 978-1492998891
ISBN-10: 1492998893

e-book ISBN 978-0-9794498-1-9

In loving memory of

Captain Leif M. Jonassen, Sr.

David A. Beil, USN

and in honor of

Captain Leif M. Jonassen, Jr.

CONTENTS

Chapter One   page 9

The Ship's History

Chapter Two   page 15

The Staff

Chapter Three   page 31

Suites, Grand Salon,
Pool & Medical.

Chapter Four   page 39

The Food Service

Chapter Five   page 45

Winston Churchill

Chapter Six   page 55

Passenger Manifest

Chapter Seven   page 63

Royal Guests

Chapter Eight   page 69
Jackie's Cruises

Chapter Nine   page 75

The Wedding Reception

Chapter Ten   page 83

The Last Onassis Cruise

Chapter Eleven   page 89

**Refurbishment
and Return to the Sea**

About The author   page 95

Bibliography   page 97

Chapter One

The History

Aristotle Onassis often quoted Socrates by saying, "The unexamined life is not worth living." He also said, "They say I have no class. Fortunately, people with class are usually willing to overlook this flaw because I am very rich. You can't buy class, but you can buy tolerance for its absence." This is exactly what Aristotle Onassis did with his life when he purchased a dilapidated Canadian frigate of warlike mien with no pretensions to grandeur whatever. Onassis recreated this sorry ship as the Christina which became "the crystallization of Ari's charm."

Before we explore the Christina's enchanted existence as the ultimate luxury yacht of its time, we must first look at the life and character of her owner, Aristotle Onassis. This man identified strongly with the Greek mythological figure Odysseus. Although he was by no means a scholar, Aristotle was fascinated by the story of Odysseus. It was about his eternal journey in search of adventure and his eventual return to his native country and people.

Onassis always felt a similar destiny and he was very attracted to this ancient Greek hero. As he embraced life with unrestrained enthusiasm and gusto, Aristotle identified with his Greek hero, Odysseus, in many ways.

Aristotle Onassis knew how to exist above all will. There was nothing that could hold him back from what he believed to be his grand destiny whether it was in business or in his private life. His stellar performance in the business world was directly tied to this part of his character. He was willing to win at any price. As he went down the path of success with the determination always to succeed, he felt that he was omnipotent. He faced his enemies, rivals and detractors with a crescendo of power that over-whelmed most mere mortals.

He had a flair and charm about himself that was incredibly seductive. His vibrant personality enchanted both men and woman alike. He fascinated people with his combined enormous ego and then with his sweet vulnerability. He literally oozed charm and charisma as he made his way through the power centers of the rich and the famous. He could be at the same time one of the most vital men alive and then within seconds change to one of the most melancholy, sad souls to ever exist.

Sadly despite all of his great success in the business world, fate was not to allow him to reap personal happiness in his private life. The story by Odysseus that Aristotle loved the most was the one that depicted the punishment of the man who had challenged the omnipotence and authority of the lords. Similar to Prometheus who in life had attained the heights, Aristotle was most like the son precipitated on the ground in the legend of Icarus. Onassis sadly spent the last two years of his life without hope and fighting without any enthusiasm.

This was the man who resurrected a Canadian frigate with the intention of making this ship, the Christina, the center of his universe. In 1953, he was laying plans that, if successful, would make him the wealthiest and most powerful man in the world, at least that was his hope. But the money would lose much of its luster if he lacked a proper forum for its display. Consequently, he eagerly entered into the purchase of a new acquisition which would be come the crown jewel of his fleet. There was another motivation behind this purchase by Aristotle Onassis and it was simply one fierce on going competition with his brother-in-law, Stavos Niarchos. They were to become life long rivals in every area of their business and personal lives. All really rich men had yachts and the richer the man the more splendid his vessel. If Niarchos had a grand ship that was grander. It was just a fact of life and it certainly made for interesting family gatherings.

The yacht that has become world famous known as the Christina had a very ordinary beginning as far as vessels go. It was formerly a war-surplus, 1,800-ton Royal Canadian frigate called the Stormont. It was purchased by Aristotle Onassis in 1953. An American racetrack owner made the Stormont available for only fifty thousand dollars. Ari eventually spent over four million dollars to have her gutted and converted into a pleasure craft. One writer subsequently called the ship, "a three-hundred-and-twenty-five-foot hull of dazzling indifference to the outside world." This refurbishment took place in Kiel, Germany under the direction of Caesar Pinnau, a German professor of architecture. Pinnau had also designed Adolph Hitler's mountaintop hideaway near Berchtesgaden.

The specialists at Howerke-Hamburg labored under only one constraint, Mr. Onassis demanded perfection in all things concerning this ship. When he detected ripples where the rakish new bow joined the hull, he ordered it torn off and the work redone. Inspecting the ship one day with Kurt Reiter, he discovered knots in the wooden screening that covered the metal bulkheads. This screening that would disappear behind oak paneling, he ordered it replaced immediately. The Germans, who were used to Onassis' usual indifference to the construction of his tankers, found him to be exceedingly trying during this refurbishment.

Onassis acknowledged to Kurt Reiter that the ship was a rich man's toy but he took it very seriously. He was infuriated by any suggestion that Niarchos' graceful three-mast schooner, the Creole, was somehow more of a real yacht and, by extension, that his arch-rival was a real sailor.

The Christina looked like a fabulous villa, but in turbulent weather things could become rather dicey. She was sullen, sluggish and awkward enough to worry the most seasoned of sailors. Probably because he reasoned that the vibrations of a powerful motor would damage his objects d' art on board, Onassis decided to retain the Christina's original steam engines with the result that her top speed was only fourteen knots. According to Captain Kostas, the ship was capable of going 18 knots but he stated, "We rarely approached that speed because great vibrations resulted when we tried. Our maximum speed with guests aboard was fourteen knots."

Worse still, another deck was added, making the vessel proportionately too high for its length. So in rough weather, the ship is like a sailor without his sea legs. Before the renovation, Onassis was warned that adding the third deck, the hydroplane, and the crane would make the ship top-heavy and very risky to pilot in a storm. Consequently, the yacht's design included stabilizers that were extended to keep her steady in rough seas. It was completely refurbished three times in Germany before it met with Onassis' exacting specifications.

The ship was launched in Hamburg and named after his daughter, Christina, who was three years old at the time. This was the only ship in the Onassis fleet for which he felt such a deep affection that it transcended the balance sheet. Whenever Ari sought validation of his status in society, he could take comfort in the Christina. The international guests that would cruise on her gave Onassis an index of his own standing.

Shortly after the Christina's launching, Onassis heard that the West Gennan chancellor, Dr. Konrad Adenauer, was anxious to meet the man who had done so much to revive his country's shipping industry. Onassis met the chancellor at the Palais Schaumburg in Bonn and made an excellent impression. As a business acquisition, the Christina was one of the best investments that Onassis had ever made. It opened doors to him that had formerly been shut and raised his enterprises to a higher level.

When it finally was ready, the Christina sailed under a Liberian flag. The maiden voyage took place in June of 1954. The ship was sleek and streamline, pristinely white with a bright yellow funnel. The ship was 325 feet long with a water displacement of three thousand tons.

Aristotle Onassis often told his friends how as a young, penniless boy he had sailed in steerage class to Argentina. He had vowed then to better his circumstances and now his dreams had come true with the ownership of the magnificent Christina. It was the floating palace of his dreams. He had replaced the short, dark haired, penniless little boy who had walked off a refugee ship with a man who was to become a legend in his own time. He had amassed a fortune that was estimated at five hundred million to one billion dollars, owned homes and apartments on three continents, controlled a fleet of over one hundred ships and lived like a medieval king on his own private island, Skorpios, in the Ionian Sea. He courted and successfully had affairs with some of the most glamorous women in the world and owned a Casino in Monaco just for good measure.

Onassis frequently did business with the most influential men in the world and was on a first name basis with most heads of state. He wed the daughter of the wealthiest man in Greece, lived openly with a world famous opera singer and then eventually wed the widow of the president of the United States.

Once asked the formula for success, Onassis replied: "work twenty hours a day, be willing to take risks, lend and ear to important gossip, and offer tempting bait to get what you want." He followed his own advice and proceeded to live accordingly as his fantasies became his realities.

The reality was that this ship was his kingdom at sea. The Christina became his country of choice. It was the ultimate residence for a man who had many residences but none that he loved as mush as the Christina. She was his obsession.

The Christina was where he lived, worked and played. Onassis often said that it was his preferred residence and he would fly into a fit of temper if a single brass knob were not properly polished.

The famous yacht was the cornerstone of Onassis' reputation for decadent wealth. It became a big part of the new jet style type of living in the early fifties and sixties. It was one of the largest, most opulent vessels in the world. It was the ultimate ship to sail the high sea. As the Lord and Master of this ship, Aristotle Onassis was the King of the World.

For Aristotle, the Onassis Odyssey had reached the heights. The Christina had become the symbol of all his dreams and aspirations. He had surpassed the dreams of mere mortals and he now lived with the gods when he was aboard his floating kingdom.

Chapter Two

The Staff

Aristotle Onassis often said that the Christina was his preferred residence. It was the one place in his entire universe where he felt completely in control. The ship was his home and the place where he felt the most comfortable. This feeling of serenity was due in large part to the crew of sixty that included officers, sailors and miscellaneous staff. They were there to serve him and his guests around the clock. The Christina was Aristotle's country. It was a country ruled by a benevolent emperor who was served by a loyal and devoted crew and staff.

The staff seldom saw Aristotle during the daytime. He would be out of sight either sleeping or monitoring the movements of his ships throughout the world. Onassis controlled his empire from the two radiotelephones on board the Christina. Only after his work for the day was done would he emerge in the evening to play his guitar, and tell stories and preside over the entertainment on board the ship.

The primary crew on board the Christina consisted of Captain Kostas Anastasiades, the First Mate and Chief Engineer Sefanos Darousos along with many sailors and household staff. When Onassis rolled out the red carpet for celebrities such as Winston Churchill and Jackie Kennedy, the crew would include two hairdressers, three chefs, a Swedish masseuse and a small orchestra for dancing. There was nothing that was as good as Aristotle endeavored to impress and pamper the chosen few who were lucky enough to cruise with him on the Christina.

Whenever Aristotle Onassis came on board after a few days absence, the same ritual was always observed. Accompanied by the captain, first mate and the chief engineer, Onassis would make a very thorough tour of inspection. He was meticulous and expected the same from his crew. Since the lounge and his private cabin were always impeccable, he didn't even bother checking on them.

Instead Aristotle would pride himself on visiting the most unlikely and unexpected places. With his fingers or a white handkerchief, he would search for dust and there would be hell to pay if he found anything amiss. Sometimes, he would shout so loud and long that he would actually lose his voice for several days. His wife, Tina, once said. "That to Ari the Christina was not a fantastic plaything but a real passion. He is almost like a housewife fussing over it." This ship was his obsession even beyond passion.

One time when Onassis returned to his ship after a ten-day visit to Paris, there was hell to be paid by one unfortunate crewmember. Onassis decided he wanted to see the galleys, the engine room and the officer's cabins. Four of these cabins shared a single bathroom, which he also wanted to inspect. After carefully looking at everything, his glance fell upon a tiny spot on the carpet behind the bidet. It so happened that the drainpipe had been dripping very slowly for several days. The cabin boy in charge of cleaning the area had asked one of the handymen on board to fix it. Unfortunately the man forgot.

At this point, Onassis immediately summoned the cabin boy in question and said that judging by the deposit of salt, the leak must have been there for at least two weeks. Now because the cabin boy hadn't called anyone in to fix it, he was guilty of gross negligence. Onassis promptly gave the boy his notice, with orders to leave the ship the next morning.

There was negligence, all right, but the cabin boy wasn't the guilty party. Still, rather than inform on another crew member, the boy accepted his punishment of dismissal without a complaint.

The story didn't end there but what happened next was a typical example of how Onassis interacted with his employees. He was able to take his time and thoroughly reconsider what to most people would seem to be a fairly minor problem. He had an intuitive sense and was capable of changing his mind.

After dinner the same evening, Onassis went out on the main deck and began pacing back and forth. Finally he returned to the main lounge and sent for the boy he'd fired only a few hours earlier. This time he asked the young many why he hadn't reported the leak to anyone.

Still not wanting to betray the handyman, the boy said he'd simply forgotten. Now this was the worst crime you could commit in Onassis' opinion. "You forgot?" he said, repeating over and over, as he tended to do whenever he was really angry. "Do I ever forget to fulfill my responsibilities to you?"

Finally his anger subsided, and in a kind voice he told the young boy to go to bed and he would discuss the matter with him in the morning. Ten minutes later, the handyman was fired and sent on his way. No one had told him, but Onassis guessed the truth. Although it was a minor incident, it gives a remarkable insight into a most forgiving aspect of the man's character and personality.

Insights such as the previous one as to the workings of the crew and their relationships to Onassis comes to us from a former crew member, Christian Cafarkis who wrote a book, entitled The Fabulous Onassis, after he no longer worked on the Christina.

Although Onassis dismissed the book as pure fiction, it is worth noting that Mr. Cafarkis was not fired but rather left his employment with the Christina due to an early inheritance. After reading his account of life on the Christina, it appears that he had no other agenda but to tell a very interesting story. In fact, he is quite complimentary to Aristotle Onassis and all of his wives and various guests. It is a fairly objective view of the intimate nature of life aboard this incredible ship.

From this source, many interesting details of life aboard the Christina are revealed for posterity. For example, all male employees were required to be excellent dancers or at least know how to dance. Also as part of the hiring process, all men were asked if they liked women since homosexuals were not welcome aboard this ship. It also helped to be able to speak other languages besides Greek.

Upon being hired, a new crew member would quickly find out that many people referred to Aristotle Onassis as Barbas behind his back which in Greek means "uncle." It was a constant reminder that their boss was infinitely rich and powerful. If the Americans had their Uncle Sam, then the Greeks had their Uncle Onassis.

Once on board, the officers, sailors and staff had their various specialized jobs, but no one really had a single well-defined task. For example, even though a crew member might be hired to wait on tables he would still be expected to clean the dining room with a broom, mop and pail. Everyone was expected to do whatever needed to be done at any given time.

Everyone on the crew knew that they were expected to work above and beyond their regular assignments and yet they were willing to do so because they loved and respected Aristotle Onassis. He was a benevolent boss.

Many times he would say, it was no problem to help those who needed help. The hard part was to give them this help without insulting or demeaning them. Once when Onassis was about to untie his small Chris-Craft from beside the Christina, he noticed a boy holding the small boat for him. "Who are you and what are you doing here?" he yelled at the small boy. "No one can see you here. Don't you understand that it is dangerous for a boy like you to be here alone beside my ship?"

"The only thing I understand," the boy, whose name was Georgakis and who was fifteen years old replied, "is that I want to live, I need to work, and I need money." Mr. Onassis was deeply touched by Georgakis' earnestness and asked him what kind of job he thought he could do. "Any job you can find for me," the boy said. "Please take me on your boat."

After determining that the boy was telling the truth and had no family to take care of him, Onassis found him a job on the Christina. Several years later, Georgakis was employed at Olympic Airways, were he remained a deeply devoted and loyal employee until Mr. Onassis' death.

There were so many stories and examples of the kindness and concern shown to so many of the Onassis family employees. Such as the time the ship was anchored in Monte Carlo, Tina Onassis received a phone call from the woman who regularly supplied flowers for the Christina. The woman was in some sort of trouble and needed the three thousand dollars that was owed to her right away. Tina immediately gave the money to a crewman, in cash, to deliver to the florist immediately. He set off at noon, but still hadn't returned by five o'clock from an errand that only should have taken a half an hour.

The explanation was simple. While Onassis was on board worrying about what had happened to his crewman, the man was at the casino, losing all of the florist's money. Finally after he was flat broke, he returned and sadly confessed his crime.

Unbelievably it was a full six months before the crewman left the Onassis' service. Tina certainly tried to get rid of him. In the meantime, the crewman completely demolished two Ferraris that Onassis had lent him. Much to Tina's chagrin, Ari liked the man and simply did not want to fire him despite his many problems. Finally Tina fired the crewman for another transgression, when Onassis was away on a business trip to Mexico.

The Christina had many comforts and luxuries for her crew that you wouldn't find on most pleasure ships. For instance, all of the cabins for guests and crew alike were comfortably air-conditioned. Food for the crew was another matter. Despite the mountains of food and drink bought for the ship, the crew ate rather poorly. And if you had the misfortune of being Greek, you couldn't even get a drink. The crew dining room was separate into two sections by a large cream-colored screen. The Greeks ate on one side and the non-Greeks ate on the other side.

The reason for this was that 0nassis observed a law of the Greek Merchant Marine that forbids sailors to be given wine. Thus Greek sailors were allowed only a bottle of beer every Saturday and Sunday, while the French and German sailors were each allotted a half-bottle of wine per meal. The Greek sailors felt it was a most unfair situation but there wasn't anyone to complain to that would listen. This policy created fierce jealousies among the crew but it never changed, despite numerous petitions sent to the boss.

The Greek Merchant Marine was also responsible for the daily menus on board, which were the same week after week, year after year. The crew always knew that on Mondays they'd have fish, Tuesday's sausage, and so on. This was not only monotonous, but also very frustrating, especially when they watched the chefs preparing haute cuisine meals for the family and their guests on a daily schedule.

Another problem the crew had was getting on and off the ship when in port. Normally, the crew and guests alike were allowed to use the same gangway, but whenever Winston Churchill was on board, only the family, their guests and the officers were eligible for this privilege. The rest of the crew had to disembark through an opening on the port side.

One crew member related this amusing tale regarding this practice. One night in Gibraltar, he was getting ready to go ashore after work. He had to use the inconvenient side exit. The ship's carpenters and mechanics had rigged up a system of ropes and pulleys so that the crew could cross over the hundred feet or so that separated them from the dock. First he had to glide down a rope into a tiny boat the bobbed unsteadily in the water. Then he had to pull another rope that would tow this frail little craft into the dock. Tired at the end of a long day, it was a most inconvenient maneuver, to say the least.

Just as he was trying to decide how to get down without getting his white sweater dirty, as luck would have it, he found himself face to face with Onassis. He must have been on his way to check on the morale of the crew, which he had heard was low because of the gymnastics required of them to get ashore.

He turned away, hoping to avoid this direct confrontation, but it was too late. Onassis called out his name. As casually as possible, he walked over and asked his boss what he wanted. Instead of answering, Onassis stared long and hard at the crewman's sweater. He walked all the way around to the back of the man and then facing him, quietly asked where the name of the ship had gone. Onassis was referring to the name, Christina, which had been sewn onto to the sweater, given to him when he started to work on the ship.

The truth was that in order to avoid the endless questions about the private life of Onassis, the crewman had cut the letters off, so he would be unrecognized as a Christina crew member while on shore, especially by reporters. Although Onassis, had caught him, he decided to play it dumb.

"What!" he said. "You mean they aren't there anymore?"
"I guess they must have disintegrated," he replied.
The crewman was lucky that night because he got to explain how impossible it was to enjoy shore leave with the Christina name on his sweater.

"Oh, I understand," Onassis sympathized. "You're scared stiff everyone will take you for the owner of the Christina and ask you for money!"

Seriously though, Onassis was anxious to know what sort of things people wanted to find out. Only a few days before in Monte Carlo, a reporter from one of the large American monthly magazines had offered the crewman five thousand dollars to tell everything that happened on the Christina. Needless to say, Onassis was very impressed and pleased that the crewman turned it down. The loyalty of the crew was one of the things that Onassis came to depend on and delight in his entire life.

There was one guest on the Christina that the crew never grew to like or respect. Unfortunately, the person was Maria Callas who was Aristotle's mistress for many years. All of the entire staff tried hard to please Maria, but she was not an easy person to please. The fact that she was an insecure woman who, despite her great talent and fame, did not have total confidence in herself did not make their job simple. While the crew and staff were always respectful and courteous to her, many of them did not like her.

One reason for their lack of affection for her might have been that Maria never offered compliments to them. Before many dinners, she and Aristotle walked into the kitchen and sampled the food the chef was to serve, praising it loudly and passionately with each mouthful. However when she was alone, Maria never praised or thanked the staff for anything. This neglectful attitude made it difficult for the staff to feel anything but resentment towards this great diva.

Maria wasn't the only woman aboard the Christina that Onassis had problems with on his floating empire. After he married Jackie Kennedy, much to Maria's and his children's dismay, they shared many evening aboard that were not pure bliss.

One of the waiters related that while he was serving dinner to them one evening, Mr. Onassis told him it was all right for him to clear the table. Suddenly, Jackie declared, "It is not time to clear the table. I will tell you when it is."

The busboy stared at Mr. Onassis, who shrugged and told him to listen to his wife. Jackie smiled and a few minutes later, she called him back and told him it was time to clear the dishes. This time, Mr. Onassis said nothing, but he was not upset. No doubt, this must have been early in their marriage while Onassis was still enchanted with his young bride.

There were always two ladies' maids and a valet on constant call and just the touch of a button summoned the barman or any other servant. Also there were staffs called "the groundhogs," because they spent their entire life buried under large piles of laundry, deep down in the heart of the ship. It was a husband and wife team. The husband named Joseph while his wife was nameless. They were only seen at mealtimes when they would surface to eat.

They only were allowed to wash Onassis' underwear, socks and suits to clean but never his shirts. This was amazing since Aristotle was known to change his shirt as often as six times a day. The shirts were flown off the ship once a week to a special laundry in Athens, the only one he allowed to do his shirts. Whether he was in Paris, New York or aboard the Christina, his shirts were always done in Greece. The really ironic thing about the shirts was that Onassis absolutely refused to give a shirt away until it was virtually in rags, and long after the collar and cuffs had been redone several times.

There's another amusing tale about Joseph and his wife in regards to Winston Churchill's visits on the Christina. They did not look forward to his taking up residence on board. Unfortunately, Sir Winston as he aged became incontinent and had to change his clothes several times a day. This whole story ends with their departure from the ship, but not before they'd made tidy profit from a most awkward situation.

It all started the previous year. The day before the Christina was to set sail with her prestigious guests, the Churchill's, Joseph and his wife let Onassis know through the second mate, that they would not be going without a substantial raise in salary. To avoid any last minute inconvenience, Onassis doubled their salary and they happily stayed on the ship.

Then half way through the cruise, the couple decided to give notice. When Onassis found out why they were leaving due to his friends problem, he went to the laundry in a frightful rage. "You can both go to hell!" he told them. "Nobody will miss you in the slightest! I'll wash Mr. Churchill's clothes myself, if necessary!"

In fact, he would have done so, if another couple had been hired right away and brought by hydroplane to Gibraltar, where the Christina was anchored. Onassis truly felt that it was an honor to be associated with Winston and nothing was beneath his dignity just to be able to be in such close proximity to such a great man.

Interestingly enough, the original couples, with their combined savings and severance pay, were able to set up a large cleaning shop in Monte Carlo. It even turned out that they'd also weaseled money out of Churchill, which is even more incredible, since he absolutely never tipped any of Onassis' employees on the yacht.

One time when the ship was anchored in the bay and Onassis, accompanied by three sailors, decided to go ashore to discuss the unloading of some merchandize. In addition to his regular shabby outfit, he was wearing an old beret that had once been white but was quite yellowed with age.

When Onassis and the sailors landed, the dock workers who were extremely eager to find out all about the Christina and her famous owner were waiting ashore. They didn't recognize Onassis in their presence and started right in by asking, "Is the old bastard still as cheap as he used to be?" They continued on with all sorts of crude questions about his private life as he quietly listened. The speculations became more and more vulgar as the conversation continued.

Meanwhile, the crewmen tried to discreetly indicate who was in their presence, to no avail. After there was nothing disparaging left to be said about him, Onassis' only comment was, "At least I know one place were I'm well liked."

He calmly got back on board his small Chris-Craft leaving the men on shore horror-stricken when they finally realized whom he was. As he left, they belatedly had the presence of mind to snatch their caps from their heads. Onassis laughed all the way back to his ship. The reality was that Onassis was incredibly generous with all of his employees. If one of his crew needed money, if for example a member of their family was ill, Onassis would immediately advance the money. The employee would pay back in monthly installments from his wages. More often than not, after several payments, Onassis would cancel the debt altogether.

One of the best parties ever that took place on the Christina was for the couple who worked at Onassis' Paris apartment, George and Helene. Onassis was the witness for their marriage in Monte Carlo and then escorted them aboard his ship. The celebration lasted three whole days and nights. Onassis had several Greek orchestras brought over from Athens. Ten cooks were in charge of roasting lamb, fish and lobster. All of the employees of the Christina were invited. Everybody danced and had fun together regardless of social status. Very few kings or millionaires were known to go to such trouble on behalf of their servants.

Although in some ways he was an extremely easy touch, Onassis was very sensitive about people taking advantage of his generosity. Consequently, he decided to plant a spy within the crew. He chose a ship's carpenter named Achilles who had been devoted to Onassis for years. He made a daily report but there was very little material since the crew was generally on their best behavior. They behaved first because of loyalty and second because they did not wish to be fired.

One crew member who did lose his job was named Peter who wanted to impress a young girl he had met in a bar in Monte Carlo. Peter was a handsome English fellow around thirty years. Although he was a simple mechanic, he'd told the girl he was the first mate of the Christina. To prove this he decided to borrow the seldom used sky-blue Austin that Onassis parked on the dock next to the ship. At eight that evening Peter left and returned drunk as a skunk at two in the morning.

The next day at lunch he was boasting of his sexual prowess when Onassis arrived on board with the supposed object of exploits. The girl pointed out Peter whom she said had raped her the night before. At that point, Onassis fired Peter on the spot only after he had sufficiently humiliated him in front of the crew.

After that incident, Onassis told the crew that he would no longer lend them anything. Henceforth, they were required to be back on the ship either no later than midnight or no earlier than six in the morning. For months afterward, you would see many a sailor from the Christina hanging around the bars in Monte Carlo, waiting for the dawn.

During Aristotle Onassis' entire reign on the Christina, the crew and staff had to become very good at anticipating their bosses moods since it affected everyone on the ship. It was essential for things to run smoothly on board and this in turn would keep Onassis' life on an even keel. The crew was aware of everything he said and did and how it affected their lives. It was as if the entire crews were in collaboration with one goal. The goal being to please and understand the man they all served and loved.

Onassis was generally an understanding employer but there was one area were he could be rigid. He was deeply unforgiving of sloppiness on the part of the Christina's crew. He would fire men without hesitation where the captain might have just settled for a dressing down. "You could smash a $20,000 speedboat to pieces and not a word would be uttered by the boss," a former deckhand told us. "But spit on the Christina's deck and you were out of a job." There were no exceptions made to this mandate and it instilled pride in the entire crew. They were proud of their ship and proud of her owner.

Towards the end of his life and after his son had died, he went back to Scorpios for the first time since the funeral on the Christina. As if it were a symbolic gesture that the past had been buried with his son, he invited his ex-wife Tina who had married his arch-rival Stavros Niarchos to visit the grave with him. It was bizarre as their two yachts met in between their private islands. One spectator said, "It was a very strange meeting in the middle of the ocean, those two enormous yachts....as if two warlords were meeting to sign a peace treaty in neutral waters or something."

For some unknown reason, Jackie was furious. She wished Stavros hadn't come and she refused to go over for lunch on his new yacht, the Atlantis. Ari went without her and when he arrived the Niarchos crew, immaculate in white uniforms and caps, drew up in a guard of honor to greet their guests. "They weren't at all like Ari's crew, who were much more informal wearing little T-shirts with Christina written across the fronts."

Later that night, they all went to a local island for dinner, and afterward Ari invited everyone back to the Christina for a nightcap. "It was astonishing," recalls one guest. "We were met by Ari's captain and crew absolutely impeccably turned out in tropical uniforms and peaked caps. The captain wore more braid than any admiral that I've ever seen in my life. Where Ari got those outfits from in the middle of the Aegean I don't know. That's the kind of thing he would do." He was a proud man, proud of his crew and they were proud of him.

Make no mistake, his crew loved him and they loved serving on the Christina. He had so much pride in his ship and her crew and they all shared in his extravagant lifestyle. Even though his crew was on the peripheral of his life, they felt as though they were in the center of his life because that's where the Christina was. It was the centerpiece of an extraordinary life! It was his kingdom and they were his knights serving him with honor and pride. Simply put, the Christina was his country and his crews were honored to be his loyal citizens.

Chapter Three

The Suites

Egypt's King Farouk, a man who knew something about conspicuous consumption, described the Christina's interior as "the last word in opulence". There was no one who was lucky enough to be invited aboard that didn't come away totally impressed. "I don't think there is a man or woman on earth who would not be seduced by the sheer shameless narcissism of this boat," said Richard Burton. To which Ari modestly replied, "I've found that to be so."

Soon after the Christina was launched in 1954 and received the finishing decorating touches under Tina Onassis' direction, it became Onassis principal residence with his wife and children paying him frequent visits. At that time, his main headquarters were in Monte Carlo where he could oversee all of his primary business ventures from his magnificent ship.

The vessel was a stunning tool that promoted both Onassis and the principality of Monaco. The ships attention-winning splendor fed Onassis' monumental ego. Other tycoons owned estates but he was the only tycoon with a ship that had nine large guest cabins and some with their own sitting rooms.

Each of the nine suites on his ship was named after a Greek island and contained its own elegant marble bathroom. The names of Ithaki, Mykonos, Lesbos, Andros, Chios, Santorini, Crete, Rhodes and Corfu hung proudly above the door to each stateroom identified by an oval white-and-gold plaque on the door that bore a silhouette of the island with its name both in English and Greek.

Entering the hallway one first saw the smaller staterooms "Andros" and "Lesbos" opposite each other. "Andros" was the captain's room, situated so he could quickly run up to the bridge when needed. "Lesbos" was the children's stateroom, unless it was required for extra guests. When Maria Callas was on board, she stayed in the Santorini suite and made it her home away from home. Inside each room, the specific wood or stone indigenous to each island filled the room, transporting its guest vicariously to the shores of the island namesake. All the bathrooms to the suites were filled with marble and boasted ornate gold fixtures. Yet comfort was the first consideration in each of the cabins.

As fabulous as the nine suites were, they could not hold a candle to Onassis' own private quarters that were a four room master suite atop the ship on the bridge deck with the theme of the Palace of Knossos. His apartment consisted of an office, bedroom and semi-circular bathroom.

In Ari's bedroom with its king-sized bed, sea foam-green walls were lined with beveled Venetian mirrors built into arched ivory frames carved with scallop-shell designs. The furniture was also Venetian, lacquered and painted with floral motifs. Many precious Byzantine icons glimmered from the walls. In the main bedroom of the suite was a white couch, multiple mirrors, and a large bed beside which rested four saint's pictures, as well as a picture of Onassis' beloved sister, Artemis, which presided over his bed. In the painting, Artemis looked sad and forbidding, but in real life she was an energetic, outgoing woman.

After his mother died, his sister nurtured him and he was forever indebted to her. She in turn adored and worshipped her younger brother and worried about him all the time.

From the dressing room adjoining the master bath was a secret door to the radio room and chart room so that Onassis could avoid unwanted visitors by vanishing from his suite. This also enabled him to slip out in the middle of the night to place international phone calls that were necessary for his business empire.

On the other side of the master bedroom was Ari's personal study, where he kept his most valuable treasures, including his favorite el Greco, "Madonna with an Angel". The serene image of the Madonna was unbelievably flanked by mounted weapons, including a pair of golden sabers that were a gift from King Saud and Turkish dueling pistols hanging on the teak-paneled walls over a Louis XIV desk. Nearby a green jade statue of Buddha studded with rubies was perhaps the most precious object on board, certainly the most ornate. It was from this study that Onassis would often stay up all night talking on phones and monitoring his vast holdings all over the world.

Onassis private bathroom in Siennese marble, was a copy of King Minos' bath in ancient Crete, complete with a sunken bathtub lined with mosaic and featuring a flying-fish motif. The gold-plated dolphin fixtures used in the bathrooms throughout the ship spewed out hot and cold fresh water. One way mirrors ensured the privacy of the shower while allowing Onassis to observe anyone who entered the bathroom area. Obviously Onassis even when he was bathing still wanted to be able to see the precious icons and the El Greco that adorned the walls of his cabin.

The Christina was a floating museum. In the lounge, there's another El Greco, a Gauguin and a Pissarro. The dining room had a Vermeer and an interesting collection of paintings depicting the four seasons. These paintings were commissioned especially for the Christina. Tina Onassis and her two children, Alexander and Christina were the models for Autumn and Spring and Winter.

Summer was presented by a young lady in swimsuit lying on a beach with the casino of Monte Carlo in the background. Everywhere you looked on the ship, there were objects d' art. There was an amethyst Buddha, which was one of three of its kind in the world. Onassis had an incredible collection of eighteenth-century ivory boats. Lesser valuables are all over the ship such as little gold tobacco boxes, pewter platters, a jug adorned with the bust of Winston Churchill, the Steinway used by Maria Callas and even a slot machine from Monte Carlo.

Just off the game room was a bar room, where Onassis taste in decor reached the very heights of whimsy. If the decor of the bedroom implied that Aristotle identified with King Minos, the bar suggested that he saw himself as an adventurer of the seas, especially the mythic Greek hero Odysseus. Barrel of Barbados rum and sea chests hinted of pirate treasure. Large illustrated wall maps of the world and whaling harpoons were mounted nearby, and the circular bar itself was wound with heavy hawser rope. Beneath its glass top was a diorama with miniature ships that could be moved with magnets around a painted blue sea. They illustrated the development of sailing vessels from ancient to modem times, starting with a tiny antique ship bearing a flag reading JONAH -THE FIRST SHIPOWNER.

Whale's teeth were used for footrests on the bar stools and for handles along the bar, ready in case the sea got too rough or a guest's blood alcohol level rose so high that he was in danger of falling off his stool. The handles on the bar are scrimshaw, delicately carved with scenes illustrating the adventures of Odysseus. The most notorious decorating touches were the cushions of the bar stools, which were covered with the foreskins of whales killed by Onassis' whaling fleet. They permitted Ari with plenty of opportunities to inform his lady guests that, "Madame, you are sitting on the largest penis in the world."

An extravagant spiral staircase of bronze banisters and onyx baluster connected the three levels of the ship's public rooms. At the lowest level there was an oval dining room that could accommodate as many as twenty guests for a formal dinner. The walls of this room had been painted by the French artist Marcel Vertes with scenes of Tina and children frolicking through the four seasons, skating in winter, riding donkeys in autumn, sunbathing topless in summer, and riding on a flower-strewn gondola through the canals of Venice in springtime. If more than twenty people were expected, there was a reception hall on this level that had room for two hundred guests and an orchestra.

The main saloon had an El Greco, "The Ascension," and was large enough to be converted to a movie theater for after dinner entertainment at sea. Throughout the yacht a nautical theme prevailed, and there were dozens of ship models on display, including antique sailing vessels carved out of bone by French sailors taken prisoner during the Napoleonic Wars.

The Christina became a gallery in which Onassis could display the perfection of his family life and depth of his devotion as a father. A portrait of his daughter adorned the mantel in the vessel's library, and photographs of both children were scattered here and there throughout the ship. It was a testimony to the joy experienced by his fortunate offspring. Chirstina's dolls were dressed by Dior, a typical Onassis touch. However, it was never clear how she was expected to play with them. The walls of the nursery were decorated with fifteen panels especially painted by Aristotle's favorite artist, Ludwig Bemelmans. It was not really a playroom but rather what Onassis thought a playroom should be. There was an electric organ, and cupboards full of expensive toys.

It had everything except the presence of their father who was always involved with business or entertaining illustrious guests. The extravagant children's quarters on the ship were meant to be an expression of Onassis' affection for them. He regarded them as part of himself and his love for them was indisputable but difficult to understand especially for such young children.

The ship had all the latest modem technology which included radar, forty-two-line telephone and telex system, air-conditioning plant, operating theatre, and X-ray machine, emergency generator, and electronic temperature controls to ensure that the water in the swimming pool was comfortable.

The ship was the state of the art when it came to conveniences and safety. The galleys were completely electric, while the storage hold was equipped with refrigerators and cold-storage rooms capable of holding several tons of supplies. Safety was a paramount consideration. The hydroplane was always fueled and ready to fly at a moments notice. There were six lifeboats on the upper deck, four Chris-Craft and two smaller vessels.

The swimming pool with a mosaic floor copied from one in the Palace of Knossos that showed Cretan athletes vaulting over the back of a bull. A system of water fountains with colored lights danced at the rim of the pool, and the floor could be raised hydraulically to become a dance floor. One of Ari's entertainments was to set the dance floor descending gently when dancing was proceeding, with brightly illuminated jets coming from the sides. During the daytime a long green canopy protected the rear sitting area on the deck around the mosaic pool-cum-dance floor where guests would gather all day long and take casual meals in good weather.

On the deck below Onassis' suite, guests driven from poolside by chilly weather took refuge in the large oak-paneled game room. It was lined with bookshelves full of gilded, leather-bound books in several languages, mostly Greek history and mythology, art books or detective novels, and, of course, the complete works of Sir Winston Churchill, all personally signed to his friend Aristotle. The focal point of this room was a fireplace of brilliant lapis lazuli and on either side of it stood two cloisonné and bronze temple lions from China's Yuan dynasty, whose open mouths Onassis liked to use as ashtrays. The rugs were the finest produced in his native Smyrna. A Steinway grand piano stood in the corner waiting to be played.

Understandably, some guests found the decor of the Christina over the top, among them was Jacqueline Kennedy Onassis who was eager to re-do the ship just as she had done with the White House with her famous decorating skills. Ari was adamant that the ship was off limits to his new wife but she talked him into letting her replace the upholstery on some of the sofas, but he agreed only to temporary slipcovers that could be taken off whenever Jackie left the ship.

The Christina was the ultimate playhouse for the man who created paradise. No home could ever compete with this ship for his affections and devotion. Aristotle's favorite place was on the main deck, sitting in a comfortable chair by the pool, staring out to sea. Here he was a small man dressed in the simplest clothes, a short sleeved shirt and baggy pants, smoking a Havana cigar and drinking his ouzo. He was completely oblivious to the opulence around him. There's no denying that he craved and adored luxury but, he was basically a simple man. At the end of the day, it didn't take much to make him happy. The ship was his creation, and the Christina, with the waves of the sea lapping up against her sides, kept him happy and contented whenever he was with her.

Chapter Four

The Food

When it came to wining and dining his guests, Aristotle Onassis was the most gracious, generous and giving host in the world. There were no limits to his bounty and he loved sharing it with all of his visitors on the Christina. Good food, good friends, and good fun were the formula that he used to create an atmosphere that was very congenial. You had to experience it to believe it. He was capable of impressing the most sophisticated and jaded of guests.

If the furnishings and interiors of the Christina were thought to be extraordinary, then they were nothing compared to the amenities aboard and, in particular, the food. With two chefs always in attendance, the meals on the ship were equal to those served in the finest restaurants. Breakfast was a simple meal served whenever the guests arose, on the deck or in the stateroom or dining room whichever location was desired. Lunch was most often a beautiful buffet of foods flown in from other countries, offering choices of fishes, meats, lush vegetables, salads and fruits. Dinner was more formal, served in the dining room, with one long table on a stunningly perfect gold carpet. There were expensive wines, imported caviar, choices of main courses, and fabulous desserts that were prepared at each table. There was nothing left to be desired.

The two chefs prepared both French and Greek specialties simultaneously with most guests choosing the latter in deference to their host. As for Aristotle, his favorite dishes were raw onions liberally doused with olive oil, stuffed tomatoes and baked eggplant called papatsakia which was cut lengthwise and baked covered with onions, cheese, celery, tomatoes and peppers. This was all washed down with Dom

Perignon champagne, and he would follow his main meal with cognac, usually Courvoisier. Aristotle did not like heavy or greasy food and preferred fish and game to the heavier meats. If he ate meat, all of the fat had to be trimmed off. He was not a big eater. At the cocktail hour on board ship, his preferred drinks were ouzo and mezes rather than more elaborate concoctions.

The irregularity of his life made him prone to indigestion. Sometimes he omitted breakfast altogether, and when he took the meal it was invariably light with French coffee, scrambled or poached eggs, and fresh figs.

Onassis occasionally would slip down to the crew's mess and sampling what they were eating before dinner was served to his guests. He would reappear, exclaiming in delight at the taste of this dish and the delicacy of that. Everything served on the Christina had to be the absolute best. The finest wines were purchased and served by a sommelier that traveled on the yacht.

The quantities of food and drink that were taken on an average cruise were staggering. The cook on the ship estimated the following figures for a two week cruise: at least ten whole veal roasts, ten baby pigs, ten lambs, six roasts of beef and about two hundred chickens. It was customary to have chicken every Sunday on the Christina. As for fish, he estimated about five hundred pounds, plus around fifty lobsters and several eels for good measure.

The one thing never needed to take along was bread. Until 1961, it always arrived by plane. It seems that one day while eating in a Paris restaurant, Onassis fell in love with the bread regularly served there. Right away, he obtained the name of the baker, who was located on the corner of Victor Hugo and rue des Belles-Feuilles.

When he was in Paris, all Onassis had to do was send his chauffeur, Rozas, to buy the bread. But since he was seldom there, he devised a complicated system to fly it fresh to wherever he was. Everyday, Rozas would buy the precious bread and then deliver it to Orly Airport and put it on the Olympic flight that had landed the closest to where Onassis would be that day. When Onassis was on the Christina, George Kuris, the hydroplane pilot, would pick it up at the nearest airport.

Finally in 1961, Maria Callas who had been with Onassis on the ship for two years by then, suggested that it would be more economical and efficient to send the cook, Clement Miral, to Paris to learn how to bake the bread. From that time on, Miral held the title of chief cook and baker until Jackie Onassis discovered that the sister of Nikos on the island of Lefkas made a certain bread that was absolutely "darling-darling." When Jackie's favorite bread was brought in by plane, it was estimated that on some days the bread must have cost two hundred dollars. The nearest airport to Lefkas is Corfu, which means that a ship or plane would first make the round trip to the airport and then the bread was sent to Athens, where it would be put on an Olympic Airways plane. Although this might seem rather extravagant, it was just a minor logistic detail for Onassis. He simply wanted his family and friends to have the best.

Generally Aristotle was easy to please but the staff knew that he was also very particular about how he expected to be waited on. One crew member related a typical story in this regard. It seems that he was new on board and eager to learn the habits and idiosyncrasies of his new boss as quickly as possible. This was no small task. The first run in was over the serving of an orange. Onassis was very proud of his oranges, which came from his own garden in Glyfada. Every week an

Olympic Airways plane brings him several crates, no matter where he happened to be in the world at the time.

It was about 11 P.M. when Onassis saw the crew member on the deck and asked for an orange. It was his first private assignment for the boss and he headed happily for the galley, picked up the best orange that he could find and placed it on a plate. Proud that the whole operation hadn't taken more than a couple of minutes, he dashed back to present the prize. Onassis took the plate, glanced at the orange, frowned and then started his tirade. He wanted a knife and he wanted it right away. It was the little things that mattered and were the most important to remember when you were working for this man.

With these great quantities of fabulous foods and drinks served on a daily basis, how did they keep in shape you may wonder? Well Jackie Onassis was never heard to complain on the Christina about gaining weight or eating too many fattening foods. She displayed excellent self-control at mealtimes and rarely let up with her exercise regime. Swimming in the Christina's swimming pool or the waters of the ocean meant more than a mere dip in the water for Jackie. It meant a long, serious swim guaranteed to use up many calories. She also enjoyed water skiing off the ship, managing to stand up on the top of the water for much longer periods of time than most guests.

As for Onassis, he smoked very heavily, cigarettes during the day and a good cigar after dinner. His favorite cigars were Monte Cristos. He sweated profusely and the large handkerchief he always affected in his suits was functional as well as decorative. Aristo, too, enjoyed swimming usually in the ocean, to which a special slide from the yacht delivered him to the water for his swim, which often lasted an hour and a half at a time. He rarely took exercise for its own sake but truly enjoyed swimming. He used to say that it gave him a chance to be alone and think his own thoughts. The privacy and solitude of swimming alone was a real treat for him.

As with most extravagant operations, pilferage was always a problem on the Christina. With the exception of the works of art, almost everything else disappeared. Whiskey, champagne and a wide variety of rare liqueurs, and food were taken by the crew from the hold of the ship and resold to individuals or shopkeepers at unbeatable prices. In general, supplies of salmon, crab, lobster and shrimp were subject to inexplicable losses. One crew member wore a raincoat three sizes too big in order to hide the daily bounty of spoils collected from the ship. The only delicacy that wasn't popular with the help of their clients was white rat, although it seemed that prepared with wine and onions, it was delicious, or so they said.

Finally one day, Onassis trying to bring this deplorable situation under control, scrutinized the garbage cans, which were left out on the dock. Then at two o'clock in the morning, all hands were awakened and told to assemble in the dining room. Onassis was there, walking up and down, studying each and every crew member with his piercing eyes. He then let go with all his fury. "You're nothing more than a bunch of crooks! There are millions of starving people all over the world, and you throw anything and everything into the garbage! You'll soon see what kind of garbage you'll have to eat from now on!" He had found some enormous cuts of meat, pounds of leftover lentils and masses of fresh bread. The staff had prepared the menus authorized by Onassis, but sometimes they as much as tripled the quantity, which accounted for the terrific amount of waste and pilferage.

This man was truly a paradox. He could be the most extravagant man alive, and then become the most penny-pinching being on earth. He was hardheaded but softhearted all at the same time. His greatest pleasure came from entertaining and delighting his guests with the most fabulous foods and fine wines ever served. To Onassis the most cherished thing was to be able to serve a truly gracious meal. It was a universal gesture of friendship and hospitality.

Chapter Five

The Statesman

Up until he married Jackie Kennedy, Sir Winston Churchill had been the crown jewel of Aristotle Onassis' collection of valuable and desirable people. Entertaining and eventually becoming close friends with this statesman was a feather in Aristotle's cap that he savored all the days of his life.

One must understand that Onassis had grown bored with collecting fine art and jewelry with his great wealth. He now was into collecting people. It was all a part of his great drive to use his wealth to further his personal and business enterprises. And there was no greater catch out there, than Sir Winston Churchill. With his great prestige and impeccable reputation and credentials, Aristotle literally was foaming at the mouth with the anticipation of entertaining this great man.

It all came about when in the summer of 1958, Onassis cultivated the friendship of Randolph Churchill who effected an introduction between his father, Sir Winston, and Onassis. Sir Winston and his wife, Clementine, were holidaying on the Riviera and accepted an invitation to lunch with Onassis in Monte Carlo. There was an instant rapport between the two men. "We talked all through lunch, discussing politics, history, human affairs, and human nature," Onassis related afterwards.

A few days later, Sir Winston came to lunch on the Christina for a day trip. The entire band accompanied him from the Hotel de Paris, which Onassis borrowed for the occasion. Even though there was the provision that there be no press, when Ari came down the gangway to greet "the biggest fish he had netted so far" a swarm of photographers were there. They were there to get their pictures and file their stories. Churchill, who had difficulty getting up the gangplank, was visibly upset by the presence of so many cameras. It was a betrayal of trust, although the perfectly chilled Dom Perignon and bowls of caviar secured Churchill's quick forgiveness. Ari knelt at Winston's feet and spoon-fed him as one would a small child.

This excursion was followed by invitations to cruises aboard the Christina, eight in all from 1958 to 1963, for the Churchills. Anthony Montague Browne and Browne's wife, Noel, who was known as Norne, always accompanied Sir Winston.

Onassis' entree to Churchill had come faster and more easily than he had ever thought possible. Thus began a remarkable friendship from which they both received great pleasure from during the final seven years of Churchill's life.

There was definitely a certain amount of celebrity hunting on Onassis' side of the friendship. He basked in the exalted company that surrounded the Churchills. They were the real thing. They were unquestionably people of real class. When Churchill was aboard, the Christina would be met in foreign ports by ambassadors, governors, prime ministers and even royalty. When Churchill was aboard, you could see a change in Onassis. He was very different, no longer just a great millionaire, he was now almost like a small boy, full of admiration and respect. His friendship with this great man was a humbling experience.

When he arrived, Churchill was always elegantly dressed, sporting a navy blue polka-dot bow tie. As he boarded the Christina, he walked very slowly and painfully. The small crowd gathered on the dock would start to applaud, and Onassis, who generally never paid the slightest attention to idle bystanders of this kind, would smile happily at them. Churchill would make a slight bow to the crowd, and then would greet the crew with a smart, "Good morning, gentlemen."

One crew member remembered him as a man with two very striking physical traits. One was that his eyes although relatively small, expressed so much strength and kindness, mixed with irony and mistrust. It was impossible to divine his thoughts. Secondly, his hands were disproportionately small in relation to his body, and he held his proverbial cigar with unusual elegance between his thumb and middle finger. In addition, Churchill always carried his black cane with the silver knob that he held between his knees when sitting. He rarely was seen without a hat, indoors or out, the presence of women notwithstanding. When wearing a white suit, he discarded his gray felt in favor of an enormous straw Panama, and occasionally even sported a naval officer's hat.

In contrast to her husband, Lady Churchill had the air of a charming and warm hearted grandmother. She usually wore simple, rather long cotton-print dresses. She had an aura of kindliness and goodwill about her. She seemed to create an atmosphere of watchful understand and discretion, somewhat like a guardian angel hovering nearby.

Whenever the Churchills were aboard, Onassis made a much greater effort to appear well dressed and often wore a jacket and tie. He even would imitate Sir Winston's neatly pleated pocket handkerchief. When they were aboard, dinner jackets were worn and Onassis allowed no one to breech this rule of etiquette.

During dinner, the only wine served was champagne. Churchill only drank Dom Perignon with his meals although he would have a glass of straight whiskey before dinner. After dinner, he would eat his cheese accompanied by a half-glass of port. These evenings with Churchill were calm and dignified, although the conversation was of necessity quite loud because the elderly statesman was quite deaf by then. After Sir Winston would retire around 11:30 P.M., the atmosphere would change as Onassis would immediately take off his shoes, tie and jacket.

The Onassis children were very fond of Sir Winston and they had nicknamed him "Grandfather of the Victory." Because he so adored Churchill, Aristotle did for him what he did for no other guest ever, he allowed Sir Winston to sleep in his own private quarters while aboard. During those visits, Onassis slept in one of the other nine suites, pleased that this most treasured guest was occupying his special suite.

A typical day aboard the Christina for Churchill would begin with his being awakened exactly at 9:00A.M. His valet would then serve him a glass of orange juice and a pot of coffee. Shortly after came a second tray with various cereals. When that was finished, a third tray appeared with a single glass of whiskey. After breakfast, he usually spent the morning in bed reading books selected from the Onassis library, and rose to dress only when it was time for lunch.

Onassis actually spent his free time during the day taking care of his special guest in every way. In return, the older gentleman was very grateful. They spent most of their time together playing cards, usually gin rummy. Sometime, as an amusement, Onassis would have the pool emptied and the bottom electrically raised to the level of the deck. Then he would put two chairs in the center so that he and Churchill could be carried up and down at will. Sir Winston greatly enjoyed this game until one day when the floor got stuck in the down position. There was no danger in this, but Churchill didn't have the strength at his age to climb out of the swimming pool himself. Onassis ordered the engineer to fix it immediately, but after fifteen minutes no progress had been made.

Everyone could see that Onassis was getting more and more frustrated by this intolerable situation, imagining the difficulty in removing his friend from the bottom. Onassis never would have shown anger in front of Churchill, however, and he valiantly made a heroic effort to keep smiling and chatting amiably.

After twenty minutes, he summoned the engineer, Kimon, and spoke to him rapidly in Greek.
"How many stripes on your hat?"
"How many?"
"How many stripes on your freaking hat?" Onassis replied.
"Uh-four, sir."
"You know what you can do with those stripes, don't you?"
"Yes, sir."
"If you don't fix this floor, you can jam them!"

Intrigued by the Greek word skoufos that he'd heard, Onassis repeat, Churchill asked him what it meant. "Well, it means hat!" replied Onassis. "Hat?" Churchill said frowning. "Why on earth are you telling him to put on his hat to fix the God-damn pool? Tell him to use a screwdriver!"

Of course, Churchill was well aware that Onassis had insulted the engineer and wanted to make fun of his irascible friend. The worst of it for Onassis was that Churchill's advice worked. A few minutes later after using a screwdriver, the floor slowly started on its way up again. Smiling maliciously, Sir Winston put his arm
around Ari's shoulders and walked off the platform with him.

Churchill was extremely found of Onassis. If ever they were walking somewhere together, the old man would take his arm, and sometimes during their discussion, Churchill would rest his hand gently on his friend's in silent communication. They had a bond with each other that was both loving and tender.

Once Onassis was giving Churchill his whiskey and struck by a sudden idea he asked him if he might like to try some caviar that he had just received from Iran. Gourmet that he was, Churchill didn't have to be asked twice. The barman came back very solemnly carrying the small crystal container resting on a bed of ice in a silver bowl. Churchill must have been especially tired that day because he tried unsuccessfully to lift the small piece of buttered toast, spread with caviar and onion, which Onassis had prepared. He was ready to give up altogether when he finally spilled it all over himself.

At this point, Onassis jumped to his feet, took a small spoonful of caviar and held it for his friend, who looked back at him with an expression that was a mixture of tenderness, friendship and pain. At this time Churchill was already eight-five years old, and the natural weakness of age had been aggravated by several strokes that had definitely affected his brain and motor skills.

It was sadly true that having the former prime minister on board cut down on the staff's free time, mainly because Onassis was so demanding when Churchill was aboard. Everything had to be just right. Somehow the staff was always expected to be there when the great man required something but, of course, completely invisible, so as not to disturb him. Churchill's way of saying thank you to the staff for their constant attention and service was to give everyone a personally inscribed photograph. In addition, the officers received one of his famous cigars which they all treasured.

On another occasion, Churchill, by accident, invented another game to amuse the group on board the Christina. He'd been eating a salad over by the railing and accidentally dropped his plate overboard. By chance, five or six dolphins were following the ship and started playing with the shiny dish. Delighted, Sir Winston promptly called Onassis over to witness this phenomenon and Onassis immediately sent for more plates. The waiter naturally reached over for a pile of ordinary white plates reserved for the help since he knew what they were to be used for. When Onassis saw them, he was furious and yelled, "What do you mean by bringing me these? Get my own plates!" He wanted and expected the blue-and-white Limoges service, which were worth at least twenty dollars per plate. Onassis wanted to impress his guest and show his staff how much he treasured Churchill's idea of fun.

Along this same theme, there was the incident of the baklava. It so happened that Churchill, in spite of his frequent trips to Greece, confessed one evening that he had never tasted this national specialty. As always, Onassis went on at great length praising this excellent dessert. Although the ship was headed for Athens, Onassis couldn't wait and secretly sent his hydroplane off to pick one up. That night, proud as a school boy, he had the superb cake set down before Churchill after the cheese course.

Sir Winston knew right away how to acknowledge this generous gesture. One day soon after, he stayed in his cabin all day and even took his lunch there alone. That same night, with the help of a carpenter, he was able to hang a completed painting on the wall of the lounge. This was such an incredible gift since he rarely had the strength to paint anymore. He found that his hands trembled and the long hours of concentration exhausted him.

When Onassis arrived, he didn't notice the painting, although he commented on the smell of fresh paint. Finally when he caught sight of the painting, he was overcome with gratitude.

He admired it very enthusiastically and profusely thanked his friend, knowing how great an effort it must have been to complete.

Once when Sir Winston's beloved canary escaped in Monte Carlo, Onassis organized search parties that eventually located the bird, or more probably, a reasonable facsimile in Nice. Onassis even read all of Churchill's books and attempted to discuss them with him at every opportunity. It certainly flattered the great statesman and made for some incredible discussions. He took great delight in quoting the old man, especially if there were journalists around.

On one occasion, Onassis strove to interest Churchill in his theory of historical "necessity." It was one of his favorite topics, based on his observation that where nature provided an idyllic climate and plenty of food, people were not disposed to be very energetic. He felt that some degree of adversity was necessary to spur on any great effort. On realizing that Churchill was not interested, Onassis tried to engage him with a personal observation. "You told me, Sir Winston, that your father died very young and if he had lived to your age perhaps you would not have had to struggle so hard. Your life would have been easier." To which Churchill relied, "We were different people."

Onassis plunged on, "Yes, you were different, but you wouldn't have been driven by necessity. Churchill, still unmoved, responded with a question. "Would you like to play cards instead of talking philosophy?" Onassis protested, "Not philosophy but history!" To which Churchill replied, "They are not very different, and I enjoy living on your yacht."

In general Onassis' regard for others was essentially an extension of his own self-regard. His kindness, though considerable, was reserved for those who were useful to him or whose acquaintance reflected his own glory. Sir Winston definitely fit into this category. Churchill was an adored acquisition.

In many respects, it was truly a mutual admiration society with each man despite the disapproval from some of Churchill's friends and his own wife, Clementine. "She thought that he was keeping bad company," Churchill's grandson, Winston shared this information when he said "She disapproved of rather a lot of his friends including Onassis." However there was great empathy between the two men and they shared the same broad view of the world even though it was from different vantage points. Sir Winston described Onassis as "a man of mark."

Churchill's doctor, Lord Moran, could never really understand the fascination Onassis provided for his famous patient. One of his diary entries records this bafflement, "Onassis seems a very ordinary man to be set apart. What does Winston make of him? Is it the man or the yacht that attracts him?" Actually, it was both. What Lord Moran missed was Onassis' intense quality of attention. All those who were seduced by him experienced it and were struck by it. While in his company, they felt that Onassis considered them to be the most unique and interesting people on earth. This quality not only attracted the wealthy and powerful, it made him especially attractive to women.

Onassis even took Churchill to America on the Christina. As they entered the New York harbor, it was without a doubt one of the most glorious days in Onassis' life. If he could have, he would have unquestionably made the former prime minister a permanent fixture on his ship and in his life. Onassis seemed to have no idea of how the two of them looked together, or the things being said about them behind his back. Nor would he have cared, since Onassis was never happier or more fulfilled than when he was entertaining Sir Winston Churchill on his ship. This friendship was the ultimate experience of his life and one that he cherished above all others.

As for Sir Winston, the near senile man was content to live out his days as a possession of Aristotle Onassis. He was beyond caring what others thought. He loved spending his last days on earth enjoying the incredible luxury of the fabulous Christina.

Chapter Six

The Jet Setters

Along the way to acquiring Sir Winston Churchill and Jackie Kennedy as the crown jewels of his collection, Aristotle Onassis entertained most of the famous celebrities of his era on board the Christina. They were the original Jet Setters flying all over the world at a moments notice. They played and partied like no other generation had ever done before. Anyone who was anyone eventually would arrive on the Christina. Ari's parties aboard the Christina were "as compulsive as Gatsby's," said Hollywood mogul Darryl Zanuck, a frequent guest. It was not unusual to see on his yacht as many as a dozen international celebrities. Ari's showmanship attracted all the right people. His ship was the place to see and be seen.

Aristotle was not only a celebrity is his own right, but also he was a collector of celebrities. The Christina's passenger manifest frequently included names such as: Umberto Agnelli, Hugh and Janet Auchincloss, Billy Baldwin, Richard Burton and Liz Taylor, Maria Callas, Marlene Dietrich, Bette Davis, Douglas Fairbanks, Margot Fonteyn, Malcomb Forbes, Greta Garbo, Ava Gardner, J. Paul Getty, Cary Grant, John and Jackie Kennedy, Pat Kennedy Lawford, Rose Kennedy, Jean Kennedy Smith, Teddy Kennedy, Liza Minelli, Marilyn Monroe, Stavos Niarchos, Rudolph Nureyev, Gregory Peck, Franklin D. Roosevelt, Jr., the Rothschild family, Pierre Salinger, Frank Sinatra, Tito of Yugoslavia, Jack Warner, John Wayne, and Darryl Zanuck to name a few of the chosen guests. This list reads like the ultimate celebrity hunters line-up from Who's Who of the twentieth century.

Maria Callas was with Onassis as his mistress during the era when he entertained celebrities quite frequently. Although

Maria was uncomfortable in large groups, she enjoyed small parties on board with Onassis' friends. She especially appeared to be relaxed with two frequent guests who were Greta Garbo and Bette Davis. The two American actresses arrived together since Onassis had planned a special cruise to the Caribbean for them. He was generous to Miss Garbo, in ways other than merely inviting her as his guest on the Christina. Whenever the actress was experiencing financial difficulties, which were frequent, he never hesitated to send her a large check.

When Miss Davis and Miss Garbo were visiting on Skorpios and the ship, they would spend a lot of time swimming on the beaches or in the beautiful swimming pool on board. Both of them wore dark sunglasses and covered their heads with full scarves. Unlike Maria, they always moved as if they knew they were beautiful and that everyone would be staring at them.

Whenever the American actresses visited, either alone or together, the chefs on the Christina tried to prepare all of their favorite foods. One time when Bette Davis came alone, they enjoyed spaghetti with a special red sauce with garlic, pepper, and green vegetable that the chef from the Christina made especially for the American actress.

Onassis' wife Tina summed it up with the comment that, "Celebrities are important to Ari. All of his fantasies are connected to them." Sometimes he liked to surprise a guest with a piece of information with unexpected insight into their world. Once when Margot Fonteyn was on board, she found him to be charming and a perfect host but she had reservations about any man who "never went to the theatre or ballet." Instead he preferred to discuss business with her husband. Then one evening, she was stunned as Onassis began talking knowledgeably about elevations and entrechats, fouettes and surles pointes. He even told her that he had seen Pavlova dance once in Buenos Aires when he was a young man. There was no question of Onassis not being well versed in the finer things of life.

Onassis was no stranger to the company of the famous. He had looked in on Hollywood during the war, and he was careful to live in all the right places and cultivate the right people. The company of the powerful and the notorious had always been a comforting assurance that his life was on the right track. With the stupendous efforts of his German period behind him and his fleet of tankers becoming a reality, he proposed to launch a new initiative. He intended to take the rich and the famous and dazzle them with his splendor and his wealth. For this endeavor, the Christina would be indispensable.

Sometimes it was not smooth sailing for the celebrities on board the Christina. One time in particular in May of 1958 when Gregory Peck and Greta Garbo were guests of Onassis, things got very rough. They were in the Strait of Messina headed toward Capri. The sea was calm, the sun shining brilliantly and everyone was in such a good mood that Onassis ordered the barman to put on an album of Spanish music.

Gregory Peck, who had been lying in the sun, sprang to his feet, grabbed a red tablecloth, and immediately started to play the toreador. Onassis became the bull, lowering his hands menacingly, while everyone else clapped their hands to the music, entering into the spirit of the game.

Onassis had already missed his quarry several times when Captain Schlatermund appeared with a very worried expression. Without the slightest hesitation, he went to Onassis and asked to speak to him privately. Everyone knew that if the Captain dared to interrupt Onassis, there must be very serious trouble.

In fact, the Christina was headed straight into a violent storm. Everything happened so quickly from that point on. In less than forty-five minutes, the ship began to roll and in no time at all it became unbearable. Somehow Onassis managed to get down to the engine room, shouting and asking Kimon, the chief engineer, if the ship was going to make it.

At the height of the storm, the ship rolled over a full twenty-seven degrees, which meant that the slightest incorrect maneuver could easily have sent the vessel to the bottom. Everyone was in a state of shock and absolute panic. The guests were sweating it out below, terrified and violently ill, tossed around their cabins like rag dolls.

The storm lasted sixteen hours. Finally, the sea calmed down somewhat and they were able to see Capri off in the distance. The Christina entered the harbor in all her glory to the admiration of hundreds of tourists on the dock. No one could understand why all the guests were in such a hurry to get off and seemed so happy to be on land again.

Later Onassis admitted that for the first time in his life he had been afraid of the sea. In fact, he had been sure that the vessel was going to split in two. When the experts came to inspect the ship a few days later, they declared that the stabilizers had been incorrectly adjusted. Onassis spent a total of $75,000 to have the ship repaired. This was one cruise that many of his guests would have paid any amount to have missed.

It amused Onassis to throw groups of very different backgrounds together and see what would happen. He loved to hover on the sidelines taking in the interactions between all sorts of characters. He could be as charming to a showgirl or a mistress as he was to anyone's wife.

Onassis and Maria were always thrilled to entertain Richard Burton and Elizabeth Taylor on the Christina. They were both utterly charming and Elizabeth was both beautiful and elegant. Her husband drank an enormous amount, yet he never appeared to be drunk. It was quite amazing to watch him consume so much liquor, yet still function in such a delightful way. The two women possessed remarkable but opposing styles of beauty. Miss Taylor was small and delicate and her purple eyes were ravishing and exquisite. Yet, Maria Callas' elegance was dark and piercing, part of a strong and powerful appearance that could fill any room she entered. One night when the four of them were on the ship together, they had a wonderful time. They laughed loudly at Burton's and Onassis' jokes and Maria even sat down at the piano and graciously played every song requested. Aside from the fact that eventually, Mr. Burton appeared to drink far too much, it was a perfect night.

The summer of 1959 would be a period of great change for Onassis. Who would guess that at the beginning of August that year among the three dozen guests aboard the Christina you could have found the three most important women in his life. They were all there. Onassis' current wife, Tina, his future mistress, Maria Callas, and his future wife, Jacqueline Kennedy, all made appearances aboard the Christina that fateful summer.

The Christina was setting off for a three-week cruise on August 7th. The Churchills had come aboard a few days earlier and had settled in their cabins, as was their custom, when Onassis heard that the Kennedy's were vacationing on the Riviera. He heard about their visit from Joe Kennedy the former ambassador to England.

Joe Kennedy had done business with Onassis from the 1930s and called upon his old friend to facilitate an introduction to

Churchill for the young senator from Massachusetts. Although Joe Kennedy was disliked by Churchill, due to his appeasement policies during World War II, the great man agreed to meet the young Kennedy out of respect for his host, Onassis. After asking Churchill if he would meet with John Kennedy and getting a positive response, he extended an invitation to the senator and his wife, who accepted with great enthusiasm. The cocktail party was planned to take place on August 5th.

The young couples arrived and were introduced to the Churchills. Neither of the men was impressed with John Kennedy. However even then, Aristotle was quite taken with the young, beautiful Jacqueline. She captured his interest and he personally gave her a tour of the ship. The party on board was very elegant and gay and the Kennedys left at 7:30 P.M. Jackie was not destined to see Onassis again for three years when she ran into him in 1962 while vacationing on the Riviera. Even though it was a short visit with Churchill, Jacqueline was duly impressed and shared her experience with all the other Kennedys when she returned to the states. Jackie was enchanted with the experience and told everyone later that, "The whole thing was right out of the Arabian Nights."

Meanwhile, Maria Callas and her husband, Meneghini, had come from northern Italy to board the yacht, which was anchored in Monte Carlo. No one even thought to introduce Maria Callas to the future First Lady of the United States. They were like two ships passing in the night. This was how Onassis unwittingly managed to assemble in one place his wife, the woman who was to share his life as his mistress for ten years and the woman who was to become his second wife. It was quite a gathering on the Christina and a precursor of things to come.

After the Kennedys left, that cruise became known as the "voyage of the damned." It was on this fateful cruise that Onassis and Maria fell in love and the seeds that destroyed both of their marriages were planted. Meneghini, in his memoir, called it "the tragic adventure." But to Onassis like most things in his life, it was an auspicious beginning.

After Onassis married Jackie Kennedy in 1968, one of their favorite guests aboard the Christina was none other than Frank Sinatra. He was always pleased to receive an invitation, and he was always making jokes and laughing. Sometimes, especially when Jackie asked him, he would sing a song for them. Even Alexander and Christina enjoyed Mr. Sinatra's visits and liked to be in attendance whenever he arrived on the ship.

There was one guest who did not receive a warm welcome to the Christina. Jackie had invited Rudolph Nureyev and Ari was not eager to entertain the dancer. Once he arrived in Athens, both Mr. and Mrs. Onassis avoided him. They kept him in a hotel. The excuse was that Aristotle was going to be tied up with an urgent business matter. Finally on the day Nureyev was scheduled to leave Athens, Mr. Onassis had Nureyev delivered to the Christina, where he spent the day and was flown back to Athens in time to catch an evening flight back to Paris.

The reality was that there were few Jet Setters that Aristotle invited on board the Christina that Jackie did not enjoy. Most of the time, she was very relaxed on board, and content to let Ari smoke his Havana cigars, savor his ouzo, and enjoy his guests. He would just sit there, either in one of his favorite chairs in the main living room or out on the deck, smoke his cigar and stare our to sea. Sometimes Onassis would quietly finger his fourteen orange and green rosary beads, while the most fascinating conversations would be taking place around him. It would seem as if he were in a world of his own, far away from the group gathered around him, not hearing the words that were being spoken. Yet, suddenly, after the conversation was over, he would add something that was very intelligent and thought provoking and proved that he had been listening and heard very word. Jackie would be so proud of him and would smile broadly and lovingly at him as he spoke. These were the best of times for Onassis aboard the Christina. It truly was his season in the sun.

Chapter Seven

The Royals

When Aristotle Onassis established himself as the untitled ruler of the principality of Monaco, it was his entree into the world of royalty. Certain people maintained that it was simply by chance that Onassis became a kind of second ruler in Monte Carlo. Clearly in 1952, he had no intentions of taking over a company that operated the casino, nightclubs, a beach, a bowling alley and five hotels. All he really wanted to do was to find a place to set up his offices in a country where he wouldn't be bothered by internal revenue.

Since he loved the Riviera and adored the sea, he asked his aides to find a large building suitable for his needs. He needed a place to park his boat. They suggested the old Winter Sporting Club behind the Hotel de Paris in Monte Carlo. The ancient building belonged to the Societe des Bains de Mer, a company that was on the verge of collapse due to the lack of tourists and gamblers no longer coming to Monaco. When the director found out Onassis was interested, they offered him a deal he couldn't refuse. He would move into the Winter Sporting Club and have his official residence in Monte Carlo, and become the major stockholder in the company.

When Prince Rainier married the American actress Grace Kelly in April, 1956 and made her his princess for life, the seaplane from the Christina showered the nuptial barge with red and white carnations, the Grimaldi family colors. That night a projector aboard the yacht beamed the prince's coat of arms onto the embankment that overlooked the palace and the refurbished casino. The prospective wedding gift from Onassis was much discussed and widely expected to be another yacht, or perhaps a trinket for Princess Grace in the vicinity of a million dollars. When the actual gift turned out to be a painting by Ludwig Bemelmans, people were puzzled understandably so!

Incredibly for the paltry sum of a million dollars, the entire country of Monaco was laid at Onassis' feet. He became great friends with Prince Rainier and promised to do everything in his power to raise Monte Carlo to its former glory. It only took one year to attract rich tourists again. People still remember the fabulous parties that Onassis used to host aboard the Christina anchored there in the harbor.

These parties were gala evenings planned in order to entertain the prince and princess. The boat would be ablaze with light, flowers bloomed everywhere and the swimming pool was transformed into a Roman fountain, with jets rising in graceful arcs glowing with all the colors of the rainbow.

Although most of the woman took advantage of this splendid occasion to wear everything in their jewelry boxes, Princess Grace appeared with almost no jewelry at all, wearing a simple pink satin evening gown that accentuated her classic beauty. All of the men wore dinner jackets, including King Farouk of Egypt who had an interesting adventure that evening on board the Christina.

When he got up to dance in the midst of a fast number, the king managed to drop his revolver, which he always carried tucked into the belt of his trousers. Since his rank prevented him from bending down to pick it up, the gun was soon being kicked allover the dance floor. The king finally prevailed on a waiter to rescue the gun as discreetly as possible. Apparently, the king never used a bodyguard and was considered one of the best shots in his country.

At midnight, Onassis presented a show of fireworks that lasted twenty minutes followed by water-skiers, who performed acrobatics around the ship at about fifty miles an hour, holding lights in their hands. Needless to say, all of the guests were overwhelmed with the entire evening. The next day, the royal couple presented Onassis with a special white, blue and yellow parrot in a golden cage as a thank you gift.

Onassis relationship with Prince Rainier was complicated by what would seem to be an extraordinary reversal of their roles. It was never far from the surface and was always denied in their attempts at statesmanship. Basically the prince wanted to turn Monte Carlo into a Las Vegas style operation. Aristotle wanted to restore its lost glory and create a sanctuary for the very rich. Monte Carlo was a piece of real estate that Onassis wanted to develop to the hilt with the finest hotels and the most luxurious apartments in Europe.

There was not a single quality that His Serene Highness Prince Rainier III and Aristotle Onassis had in common. If he had not been so useful, Onassis might have been the perfect person for the prince to cut down. Rainier's initial enthusiasm for Ari had waned, perhaps because they both were arrogant and this small kingdom could not accommodate both of them with their egos.

The constant newspaper references to Onassis as the uncrowned king of Monte Carlo, and the power behind the throne, did not set well with the reigning prince. Only in the most formal situations would Ari call him Prince Rainier, preferring to call him just Rainier. Among his own staff, Ari pointedly referred to him as Mr. Grimaldi. Their positions on Monaco's direction had polarized and hardened. Their last meeting before the royal wedding had been their most acrimonious. Even though they eventually had to part company, their brief honeymoon together was incredibly productive for both of them.

After his experience with the Grimaldi family, Onassis was content to keep his distance from other royals. He would occasionally entertain royals on the Christina but purely in a social atmosphere and nothing more. Some of the royals that enjoyed his hospitality aboard the ship were ex-King Peter of Yugoslavia, ex-King Farouk of Egypt, the Begum Aga Khan, Maharani of Baroda, Princess Irene, and King Saud. He loved having them visit and they added a luster to the roster of jet-setters who partied on board the Christina. For a name dropper, these were impressive names to banter about.

There was one other minor royal who Onassis made an exception for and became quite close to him. Prince Stash Radziwill was a frequent guest on board the Christina along with his wife, Princess Lee Radziwill, who was Jackie Kennedy's sister. Ari was quite taken with the younger sister and became very close to her. They were rumored to have been an item and apparently there was enough truth to this gossip to have angered Maria Callas who was then Ari's long time mistress.

Maria had seen a picture of Onassis with his arm around Lee Radziwill in an Athens nightclub and she went crazy. Then Onassis had invited Lee to cruise with them aboard the Christina. Maria disliked Mrs. Radziwill immediately and asked Aristo to send her away. When he refused, Maria went into her suite, gathered all her personal belongings and left the ship, headed to Paris. Onassis was not terribly serious about Lee, and after a few days, he sent flowers to Maria, asking her to come back. By the time, Maria returned to the ship, Lee Radziwill was long gone.

The reality was that although Onassis liked Princess Lee Radziwell, she was just a means to an end. The real trophy that Onassis desired was far more elusive and the object of his heart's desire. She far out dazzled any of the royalty he had ever entertained. She was none other than Jacqueline Kennedy, the soon to be Queen of Camelot.

Society photographer, Jerome Zerbe, said, "It was the most expensive mistake he ever made. It was indicative of a greater failing on his part. He believed that money was a more powerful force than morality. The person that Onassis really wanted to marry he couldn't. We all know who that was....Queen Elizabeth. She would have been the top. But he couldn't have her, so he settled for jacqueline Kennedy."

Chapter Eight

The Widow

Jackie Kennedy was very impressed with Aristotle Onassis and the Christina after her first visit to the ship with her husband, Jack Kennedy, to meet Sir Winston Churchill in 1959. However Jackie was not impressed enough to jump at the chance to cruise with Mr. Onassis when they met again in the summer of 1962.

Circumstances had changed dramatically for Jackie who was now the First Lady of the United States. Jackie arrived in Greece for a five day visit where she met Ari again at the villa of Markos Nomikos, another wealthy ship owner. Ari invited her to cruise with him on the Christina but Jackie gave a noncommittal answer. This nonchalance on her part only served to intrigue and tantalize Onassis' interest in the first lady.

Aristotle waited patiently for another opportunity that soon presented itself. In 1963, Jackie was again invited, and this time, distraught at the death of her second son, Patrick, she accepted. Lee Radziwill provided the connection between Onassis and her sister. She told Onassis that the recent death of Jackie's third child had thrown her into a deep depression. Onassis immediately suggested a recuperative Aegean cruise. When Lee telephoned her sister with the invitation, Jackie accepted right away without hesitating.

The president was less enthusiastic. Onassis' well-publicized problems with the U.S. government made him a less than desirable host for a first lady. A cruise might help Jackie's spirits, but it was no prescription for votes in the next year's presidential election. Thus ensued a brief and embarrassing interlude while the fate of Jackie's cruise was heatedly debated in the White House. Jack Kennedy was adamant that Jackie refuse the invitation. He even went so far as to call Onassis an "international pirate" and a playboy. However Jackie put her foot down and insisted on going. The president had no choice but to allow her to cruise on the Christina. With an up coming election, Jackie had to be kept happy. She had the potential to become a political spoiler for the Kennedy machine. They needed her co-operation and she was essential to their plans for re-election.

The cruise was a success, marred only by periodic breakdowns in the Christina's telecommunications system that made it difficult for the president to call his wife. The Christina was stocked with eight varieties of caviar, the finest wines, and exotic fruits flown in from all over the world courtesy of Olympic Airways. The crew was sixty-strong buttressed by two hairdressers, three chefs, a Swedish masseuse and a small orchestra for dancing under the stars. The First Lady occupied the principal stateroom, Chios, and was set to sail on October 1, 1963. Onassis told the mob of reporters gathered at Piraeus to witness the departure that, "Mrs. Kennedy is in charge here."

The guest list was comprised of the Radziwills and Franklin D. Roosevelt, Jr. and his wife, Susan. President Kennedy had little confidence in Lee's credentials as a chaperone and had recruited the Roosevelts to add a little respectability to the whole thing. Ari lay low. To the disappointment of the world's press, he was no where to be seen at the beginning of the cruise. He was discreet to the point of invisibility. Finally when the yacht reached Ithaca, Jackie insisted that her host join his guest and escort her on a tour complete with his enchanting interpretations of Greek mythology. He quickly shed his shyness, taking Jackie by the hand and showing her the places of his past. Photographs of the First Lady, looking extraordinarily happy and relaxed, strolling with Ari through the back streets of his birthplace, were wired around the world.

At that point, a Republican congressman made a speech in the House criticizing the presence of Roosevelt on the Christina since he was in a position to influence relations between Onassis and the U.S. maritime authorities. The President saw the same photos and called his wife on the Christina asking her to cut short the cruise, but she refused. She had always been fascinated with everything Greek and it had long been her dream to visit these places with a guide who could make the gods and myths come alive for her. Onassis was just such a guide.

The adverse public reaction to the cruise became a topic of animated conversation at the White House. President Kennedy revealed that he had informed Onassis, through one of his aides, that he would not be welcome in the United States until after the 1964 election. It did not occur to him that it was hypocritical to let his wife cruise with a man that he would not allow in the country. Or if it did, there was nothing to be done other than take the hard line with Onassis.

At the end of the cruise, Onassis gave his guest of honor a farewell gift, a token of his admiration, a stunning diamond and ruby necklace worth fifty thousand dollars. Poor Lee was crestfallen to see what her reward was for delivering her sister to the Christina. All she had gotten from the tycoon were three little bracelets that she said, "Caroline wouldn't even wear."

Whether Lee knew it or not, the cruise had been a turning point in her relationship with Onassis. Within days, Ari had become besotted by Jackie's "sense of vulnerability," and Jackie was beguiled by her host.

Meanwhile in Washington, J. Edgar Hoover had a lengthy profile prepared on Onassis. Although there could not have been much that he didn't already know about the man whom he had investigated as a spy and a criminal and who was now beguiling the president's wife. Hoover was a great believer in no-smoke-without fire theories and was convinced that the Greek was planning something. It was exactly the type of situation that appealed to his sense of evil.

When Jackie returned to the White House on October 17th, a member of the staff was heard to say, "Jackie has stars in her eyes, Greek stars." Jackie had been on the cruise of a lifetime and it was difficult to return to the reality of life in the White House. She hated politics and now it was time to press forward with the campaign to secure the White House in 1964 for President Kennedy. This guilt about her lavish holiday in the Greek Isles with Onassis is what lead her to Dallas where she witnessed the assassination of her husband and the end of their life together.

Onassis was in Hamburg launching a tanker when he learned of John Kennedy's assassination in Dallas. He immediately telephoned Lee in London. He reminded her that he had been warned not to step foot inside America for at least a year. The following day he received an official invitation from Angier Biddle Duke, the chief of protocol, not only to attend the funeral ceremony but to be a guest at the White House. He immediately flew to Washington and had a private meeting with Mrs. Kennedy upon his arrival. He was one of the few non-family guests in the mansion to be given this honor. His presence went almost unnoticed in the days of shock and mourning that gripped the entire world.

After the President's death, Onassis remained close friends with his widow. Gradually, he began to woo her. The American Public were not aware that in December 1964 Jackie flew to Paris as the only passenger on an Olympic Airways flight. She went to be with Aristotle at his Paris apartment alone for three days. In the spring of 1968, Jackie and Ari became more public with their relationship. Jackie accepted Ari's invitation to go on a second cruise on the Christina. This time the cruise was in the Caribbean. Although the gossip columnists deemed it insignificant, the Kennedys knew that Jackie had already chosen her second husband. Jackie and Ari had a lot to discuss on that cruise.

On May 25, 1968, while the Christina was anchored in St. Thomas, Captain Kostas Anastasiades was sent to the airport to pick up an anonymous but very important guest. Nervously, Ari waited behind on the yacht. He ordered the oil painting of Tina to be removed from over the fireplace. Instead, he hung the portrait of his mother.

Onassis had Jackie fly into St. Thomas to avoid a check through customs. As soon as she came aboard the Christina, she and Onassis spent a peaceful, romantic four days sailing around the Virgin Islands. Although they carefully avoided any public displays of affection, the consensus of the crew was that, "They touched often, you could sense the electricity between them."

On May 17, 1968, a week before the widow boarded the Christina, President Lyndon Johnson requested a report from J. Edgar Hoover on Aristotle Onassis. Apparently, the president was inspired to make this request by Jackie's romance with the Greek tycoon.

These two cruises, on the Christina, were the beginning for Aristotle and Jacqueline. Their romance together was conducted within the privacy of this ship away from the prying eyes of the world. It was their private world and one in which they could totally relax and be themselves. The Christina was their haven, their port in the storms that were to descend on them before long. It was a safe place to hide away and to be hidden from the view of the world. It was the home of Odysseus, the indestructible wanderer.

Chapter Nine

The Marriage

The Christina was the site of the reception after the wedding of Aristotle Onassis and Jacqueline Kennedy on the island of Skorpios on October 20, 1968. Although the announcement of this union took the world by storm and caught most people off guard, the reality was that they had been seeing each other frequently between 1963 and 1968. It had been a courtship conducted with the greatest secrecy and discretion possible. Everyone was shocked and especially their families who were not pleased with this marriage. Nevertheless, nothing could kept them from what Onassis felt was their destiny together.

The reception following the simple service on Skorpios took place on the Christina. Aristotle outdid himself on that day for his bride and their guests. The ship became a fortress that day for the newlyweds against the prying eyes of the media. The Ship was Onassis' command center as they prepared for the invasion. Prior to the wedding the press intended to land on the beach at Skorpios since under international law Ari did not own the five or six meters of waterfront. The Christina's Piaggio seaplane and Alouette helicopter were put on the security detail. As the Christina signaled from its anchorage, thirty-six photographers, most of them Greek, hit the beach. The encounter was unpleasant and it was obvious that someone was going to get hurt. Then Jackie arrived on the scene and put a stop to things. "These men have to make a living," she reasoned and a truce was arranged.

After the wedding service in the chapel on Scorpios, The wedding party and guests emerged to be greeted by a howling wind and a rain that turned into a downpour. Later, aboard the Christina the newlyweds agreed to pose for the photographers while the journalistic fishing-boats came alongside screaming for photos until Onassis and his bride agreed to pose for them too. The reception on the Christina lasted all night, with bouzouki music, dancing girls, endless champagne, banks of flowers, and enough food to feed a compliment of sailors. Before the reception, the pool journalists were invited for pink champagne on the yacht and quickly dismissed after the couple had responded to their good wishes.

The honeymoon did not last long as far as their sleeping arrangements on board the ship. One of the crew revealed that the newlyweds slept in separate bedrooms on the Christina with Jackie taking over the luxurious cabin on the ship that used to be the exclusive domain of her husband. Ari was relegated to the Lesbos suite on the deck below.

The new Mrs. Onassis did not come cheaply to this marriage. Jackie and her children cost her husband approximately $450,000 a year, which didn't even begin to take into account the extravagant gifts or the incredible expenses of their daily life. The Christina alone cost $420,000 a year for maintenance, salaries and cruises. Nor can it be forgotten the new Mrs. Onassis received $5 million on her wedding day from her loving groom. There was $3 million for Jackie and another million for each of her children. This was cash, not trust fund money which was the controlled Kennedy legacy for the widow.

During the first years of the marriage, the Christina was a haven from the public outrage against their union. They were universally condemned and it took its toll on both of them. However, Jackie was not used to taking the heat and hate mail was something she had not been exposed to during her widowhood. She had been the Queen of Camelot, universally loved by her adoring subjects throughout the world. Now, this outcry against them was difficult for her. Aristotle told his friend, Johnny Meyer, "Jackie's got to learn to reconcile herself to being Mrs. Aristotle Onassis because the only place she'll find sympathy from now on is in the dictionary between shit and syphilis." It was tough medicine to take and much easier to bear by hiding away within the safe confines of the Christina.

Life aboard the Christina with the new Mrs. Onassis was very interesting. After the wedding, on the Fourth of July, Jackie decided to cook something particularly American to celebrate the holiday. After searching high and low around the ship, she finally had to ask her husband were the galley was! For months she had walked within a few feet of it without knowing where it was.

The crew of the Christina reported that Jackie never paid the slightest attention to them. One of the crew members was up on the deck taking pictures of Skorpios to send home to his family while Jackie was sunbathing. Jackie asked what he thought he was doing there. He said the pictures of the island were to send home to his family. She immediately confiscated his camera without letting him say another word. She was terrified that he would sell the pictures to the press.

Jackie adored the privacy that the Christina afforded her. Here no one would bother her or tell her what to do. Now she could do exactly as she pleased. Security was tight, for her and her children. No one would be judging her by the clothes she wore or the speeches she gave. She never had to give a tour of the 325-foot Christina in front of television cameras or shake hands with boring diplomats and politicians. Here she could finally be her own person. She could read, learn and listen for as many hours as there were in the day. And the best part, she could buy anything she wanted and there were no restrictions on her spending whatsoever. After her years of being controlled by the Kennedys, this feeling of freedom was exhilarating for her.

While aboard the Christina, the newlyweds would often take their meals separately from each other. This was because the loud noises that Ari made while eating aggravated Jackie. So he would take a boat over to Letkas to eat his favorite foods, the grape leaves and goat cheese that Jackie detested. Meanwhile, Jackie would remain aboard watching films and smoking tiny leather-covered pipes of different colors. After years of keeping her compulsive smoking hidden from the American public, she could now indulge freely in her own private, secured world.

The couple had some rough times early in the marriage after Ari had been photographed with Maria Callas at Maxim's in Paris. Jackie flew to Paris and the reconciliation was accomplished. At that time, they decided to take a second honeymoon on the Christina to last no less than a full year. The great businessman decided to finally stop working so hard. They returned to the Christina to cruise in the Aegean.

The entire crew immediately noticed the great change in their mistress. Jackie no longer had her bodyguards and she smiled and spoke warmly to everyone on board. She welcomed the opportunity to learn to speak Greek, which she had not tried before, although her children were starting to speak it fluently.

Jackie made a tremendous effort to be the wife that Aristotle expected when he married her. She was sweet tempered, obedient and very low key. She was really trying to make the marriage work and fit into Ari's life. Mrs. Onassis was ready to take her place beside her husband in the traditional Greek way. She even started going out with her husband in the evenings. He loved going out to nightclubs and restaurants. Previously as mentioned, Jackie had stayed on the ship but now she joined in the fun and festivities.

One night in January, 1971 she decided to surprise Ari at his favorite restaurant, Nikos' on Letkas, a simple place where the fishermen of the region would gather. They would sit at long narrow tables and drink ouzo and feast on Greek specialties. When Jackie arrived, she found him having dinner, in shirtsleeves surrounded by a group of fishermen. Ari was very proud as he stood up to welcome her and had her sit next to him in the place of honor. She joined in and enjoyed the entire meal. Then the next day, she sneaked back in secret to learn how to make stuffed grapes. This interest in Greek cuisine led her to find the galley on her own yacht. She delighted in watching the chefs and chatting about the menus with them.

The most dramatic and meaningful change in the life of this amazing couple happened while they were cruising together in 1971. The Christina encountered a violent unexpected storm. At two in the morning, Jackie was so frightened that she went down to the Lesbos suite to awaken her husband. She pleaded with him to come upstairs to her suite and stay with her. With the excuse that there could be another such storm at any time, Jackie insisted that Ari continue to share her bed each night. After that Onassis seemed to be home more and more, they were a much happier couple than ever before.

One morning an employee from the Christina enjoyed telling this tale to another employee. "The night before he had been walking on the waters edge and he suddenly noticed a small rowboat moving back and forth. When he got closer to get a better look, he saw the naked back of a man. It was Mr. Onassis and underneath him was an equally naked Mrs. Jackie. That boat was really rocking just like it was caught in a storm. When he finally left the beach, it was still rocking and the sounds of the waves could not be heard above the sound in the boat."

During the first years of their marriage, although Ari and Jackie often were surrounded by family and friends on the Christina, they were just as happy to be alone. They loved to have the ship to themselves and not have to bother with any guests at all. It would be their special time to travel to the nearby islands, especially Ithaki, the legendary home of Odysseus, Ari's favorite Greek hero.

Ithaki was a small, quiet island close to Scorpios. It was Ari's favorite place to rest and relax and in many ways seemed to be his adopted homeland. Often he would quote lines from the Odyssey for Jackie as he surveyed the island. He loved to recount the travels of his idol, the indestructible wanderer with whom he strongly identified and tried to emulate.

Often sitting on the deck of the Christina, Jackie dressed casually in shorts and a T-shirt would sit by Ari, sketching pictures of him. She would sketch him talking on the telephone, relaxing in his chair, pacing on the deck or just listening to the waves hitting the sides of the ship. He loved her humorous drawings of him and he would study every detail and comment and gently critique her work. He would be very flattered by her attention and complimentary sketches.

One day after looking at her work, he walked back to his deck chair and said, "I did not know I married a great painter." At which point Jackie put her sketchbook down and jumped up going over to kiss him saying, "And I did not know that I married a man with such a perfect appreciation for great art." Together they warmly embraced laughing and loving the moment.

Since they were such different people, it was inevitable that they would have their disagreements. They were not always the happy honeymooners during those first years. Often Ari's idea of a perfect day would be to repeat what he had done so many other times. He liked to eat in the same restaurant he dined in nearly every day, to sit in the same chair, and order the same meal he usually ate. On the Christina, he liked to swim in the pool, eat his dinner in his favorite chair, and spend the evening smoking his cigar, listening to classical music, staring at the moon and drinking his ouzo. He was a creature of habit and contented when his life followed a prescribed ritual.

Jackie craved changes. Thus conflict arose in their style of living. She was rarely happy to sit in one place and do the same thing over and over. She loved to constantly re-decorate simply because it energized her and gave her purpose. She was never happy with the status quo.

When they were on the Christina, she would badger Ari to go in after dinner to watch a movie. He preferred to sit on the deck and watch the stars in the sky rather than the ones on film. It was a constant struggle between them and it kept things interesting for both of them. It wasn't really a power struggle but rather a control issue, and they both liked to win.

They had started out with such high hopes and, yet, this marriage turned out to be a complete failure. The reality was that the marriage was only good for two years, and then things began to fall apart. Jackie started to travel again, and do her own thing. She needed to be in New York with her children, and she and Ari were no longer compatible. The glow was gone.

Especially so after the loss of his son, Alexander, in a plane crash, Onassis wanted to be alone on the Christina. Ari felt that his only son's death had been his punishment for his god-defying arrogance in marrying Jackie. More than ever, the ship became his refuge, his sanctuary. It was here that he felt the safest and where he was in total control. His home away from home had, in fact, become his only home. The Christina became the center of his universe.

Chapter Ten

The End

Aristotle Onassis lost the will to live when he lost his son, Alexander. It was the most difficult time of his life and there was nothing that anyone could do to help him. Jackie tried to do her best to help her husband weather this unbearable loss. She even organized a cruise that February, 1973 from Dakar to the Antilles and invited Pierre Salinger, JFK's former press secretary, and his wife to distract Onassis from his grief. After he had spent hours talking to Salinger about politics, journalism, and philosophy, he seemed to feel better. However after everyone else would retire in the evening, Ari would roam the decks talking to himself and grieving, not to return to his suite on the Christina until the dawn.

Onassis had a long history of talking to himself but now, due to his grief, he was getting out of control. Prior to the tragedy, Onassis would spend hour upon hour alone on the deck asking out loud all the questions that he might have to answer before going to a meeting or appointment. He would answer everything as though he had an actual audience. Sometimes he would take a few seconds to think over a reply, other times he would answer very rapidly, pretending to get angry. He would even practice saying nothing, merely nodding his head in reply to imaginary questions. He would rehearse his lines just like an actor, and try to anticipate and outguess his opponents. However, now it was not a mere matter of answering a question. Now Onassis was asking the questions and the gods were not answering.

That summer when the Christina returned to Skorpios, Onassis would spend most of his time sitting by Alexander's grave talking to his dead son for hours. He told his staff that he would often hear his son's voice. To Jackie's surprise and dismay that summer, Ari invited his former wife, Tina, and her husband, Niarchos, to visit the grave of Alexander. Before the arrival of the Niarchos yacht, Ari restored Tina's portrait to its place of honor in his study. The two yachts met at sea and proceeded to Skorpios together. Aristotle led Tina to the gravesite, where she collapsed in tears and they both mourned together. Their grief was unbearable.

In October of 1973, the tanker business collapsed throughout the world due to the OPEC oil squeeze. This did manage to distract Onassis from his grief. He decided that the key to the oil crisis was Egypt's Anwar Sadat and he intended to become acquainted. Having no introduction to the Egyptian leader, he arranged his own. That fall Onassis planned a cruise on the Christina and sailed into the Alexandria harbor, with the globally impressive Jackie at his side. The Sadat's daughter was going to be married within a few days after the Christina's arrival so the Onassis' sent a wedding gift. Then they were, of course, invited to attend the wedding. They reciprocated by inviting the entire wedding party to the Christina for a lavish dinner party.

At the time, it was said that the Egyptian cruise was orchestrated by Jackie and Christina to distract Aristotle from his grief. However the trip was pure business, a classic Onassis invasion and conquest. It would be one of the last triumphant voyages made by the Christina with Onassis in charge.

In the spring of 1974, Aristotle was diagnosed with myasthenia gravis, a degenerative muscular disease, with the primary effect being chronic and extreme fatigue and the gradual inability to control facial muscles. Basically, it was an incurable disease. It was the beginning of the end for Onassis and his empire.

It was now time for Aristotle to re-write his will and make his final bequests to his heirs. He established a foundation in the name of his dead son, to promote activities, for the most part in Greece, and to make annual awards. In regards to his yacht, the Christina, he wrote if my daughter and wife so wish, they could keep her for their personal use. If they find it too expensive to keep, estimated to cost at least $600,000 a year to maintain, they were to present it to the Greek state. A similar clause covered the future of Skorpios. Jackie was to have a 25 per cent share in both the island and the yacht.

In February of 1975, Onassis checked into the American Hospital in Paris for a gall bladder operation that was successful but left him a very sick man. He finally died on March 15, 1975 with his daughter, Christina, at his bedside. Jackie was in New York and returned to Paris immediately.

Upon hearing the news, Jackie made two phone calls. the first one was to Ted Kennedy who would be an ally in her over her share of the Onassis estate. The second call was to the designer, Valentino, since she needed a new black dress to wear to the funeral.

The body was flown to Greece and the funeral took place on Skorpios where Aristotle was buried next to his beloved, Alexander. When the ceremony ended and the crowd was milling around waiting for a sign from Christina, she told her father's closest aide, Costa Gratsos, that she wanted the island's staff and the ship's crew to assemble on the deck of the Christina, where she would speak to them. As word passed around quickly, everyone moved reverently towards the yacht.

There the Christina sat silently, serenely in the harbor that Onassis had dredged to berth her. The ship had never looked more majestic with her dazzling whiteness in such contrast to the gloomy day. The air was filled with sadness and solemnity.

This magnificent vessel had once ruled the seas and hosted all the famous celebrities of the past century. It had enthralled the world with its opulence. Now it was a ship without its captain, its reason for being no longer existed. The lonely wanderer had come home. The Onassis Odyssey was over.

Everyone gathered around to hear what the new owner would have to say to them. Throughout the ship's glorious history, this young woman had lurked in the background. Although the ship was named for her, she never felt it was hers until now. With her father who had created this vessel lying dead nearby, the ship seemed absurd, ostentatious and out of place. On the aft deck, Christina Onassis stopped as the mourners crowded around her. She began to speak, but realizing that many could not see her, she started to climb on to a large table. Arms shot out to help her, but with a gesture of dismissal, she mounted the table unassisted.

When she spoke, she knew that everyone expected to hear a daughter's homage to the father who had affected all their lives. They expected a tribute to the man who had seized the world's respect with his ascent from the depths of poverty to the pinnacle of great wealth. They expected her to eulogize the man who had conquered corporations and governments and had charmed the world's leaders and artists. They expected her to speak of his Greekness, his humor, and his generosity. They wanted to hear about the human side of the man, which was so often overshadowed by his business accomplishments. Now was not the time to praise his cunning and coups, but rather his simplistic, successful approach to life. It was the time to touch their hearts and soothe the sorrow in their souls.

As the sun set and the breeze began to blow off the Aegean Sea, the heiress, the sole survivor of the dynasty, stood on the deck of the Christina and told her father's loyal crew and all his devoted employees gathered around her, "This boat and this island are mine. You are all my people now," as she wept in front of them she continued, "I have no one else." Nothing else was said, there was nothing left to say.

She was set to take charge. But she had yet to read her father's will. She would first have to deal with his widow, Jacqueline. This would be a difficult task at least, or rather, at worst.

After her father's death, Christina would on many weekends pull herself together and arrange for elaborate parties for her friends on Skorpios, wildly drinking, singing and dancing without shoes till all hours of the night. For each moment of her guest's visits, she would have activities planned and always culminating with lavishly prepared meals on the Christina. At the conclusion of these lavish days on the ship and when her guests departed, Christina was always left alone. It was at these times that she felt a terrible melancholy. When she was alone on the Christina, the memories were too painful to bear.

In 1978, Christina invoked a clause in her father's will and gave the yacht that had born her name to the Greek state for the use of its president. She had no interest in keeping the ship and eagerly gave it away, saying, "She didn't much care for boats."

The reality was that the Christina symbolized the most exuberant, zestful time of her father's life but for his daughter it was different. She would later say that the period during which the Christina was her principal home was the least happy time of her sad childhood. When she was aboard the Christina, she was surrounded by strangers and her father was totally distracted. As a child, she was isolated in her father's adults-only world. She would be aboard the ship with her father for days, and never see him as he kept to himself closeted in his front-bridge office only to emerge to dine in state with his celebrated guests at adults-only dinners. The Christina was a place of sad, lonely memories for its namesake.

Once the ship was deeded over to the Greek government, the Christina, with its flags lowered, sat silently as her moments of glory were coming to a close. One could almost see Aristotle standing on the deck of his glorious ship, dressed in his shorts and open shirt, the wind blowing through his hair, the sun shining on his head, cigar in his mouth and a glass of ouzo in his hand. He would just be staring out to sea, enjoying all within his sight, the captain of his ship the master of his universe.

At one point in his life, Aristotle revealed that he was thinking of "making a book" about his life. When asked what kind of book he had in mind, he said that it should read like a novel. Ari thought his life's story would be a great "goddamn thriller." When asked if he imagined himself as the hero, Ari laughed loudly and replied "No, No....the villain. Villains always have the best parts." Unfortunately, the world never heard Ari's amazing story of money and mystery in his own words.

Chapter Eleven

The Return

In 1988, Tauck World discovery arranged for the purchase of the Christina and resold her to John Paul Papanicolaou, an Onassis family friend and shipping industry leader. Papanicolaou and a group of investors working together with Tauck began the Christina's unprecedented $50+ million, three-year restoration. This effort involved meticulous research, engineering and craftsmanship. Experts in yacht refurbishment have passionately restored the spacious yacht to its former glory. They have succeeded in providing today's guests with the same experience enjoyed by former guests from previous decades past.

The refurbished ship is now called the Christina O! She now takes to the sea again defining a new category of luxury yachting. The ship has undergone the most extensive restoration of a private luxury mega-yacht in maritime history and is the first to bear a passenger classification.

As her legendary past blends into the dawning of a new era, the Christina 0 affords a first-time opportunity to experience the extraordinary lifestyle of the Onassis years replete with the modern touches of the 21st century. The magnificent yacht includes 18 staterooms, all named after Onassis' favorite Greek islands. The extraordinary Onassis Suite is still the centerpiece of the yacht. It is comprised of three rooms, which include a large bedroom, bathroom and study, totaling 678 square feet. The Onassis Suite provides the ultimate luxury shipboard accommodations with panoramic ocean views. The bedroom features a king-sized bed covered in fine Venetian linens, custom made furniture from Milan and Onassis' original Baccarat crystal wall lights.

The wood-paneled study on the ship features the original onyx fireplace, leather furniture and handmade Austrian lamps and a writing desk with silver-embossed stationery. In the bathroom, which is complete with double sinks and a bathtub with six-head shower, LeFroy Brooks fittings complement the original rare marble finishes. The Onassis Suite features three large walk-in closets, two surround sound stereo systems with DVD and CD players and televisions.

Each of the other staterooms, with dimensions ranging between 150 and 236 square feet, are named after Greek Isles. The stateroom features include either a double bed or two twin-sized beds with fine Venetian lines, a seating area with antique prints of the Greek Islands, leather in-laid secretaries, mirrored walk-in closets, surround sound stereo systems with DVD and CD players along with incredible views of the sea. All bathrooms feature six-head massage showers. The Christina 0 can easily accommodate and host events for up to 100 guests using interior facilities and up to 250 guests in the canopied deck spaces.

This yacht that was famous for its magnificent parties of the past continues to amaze and amuse present day guests. It is the once in lifetime opportunity to step back in time and relive those extraordinary, extravagant events from the past. Events that we have only heard of can now be recreated in an exclusive environment at sea.

Ari's Bar is perhaps the most famous spot on board. It is where John F. Kennedy first met Sir Winston Churchill in 1957. Also, it is where Aristotle Onassis first met Jacqueline Kennedy on the same fateful day in history. The intricately detailed bar contains barrels and sea chests hinting of pirate treasure, whaling harpoons and an illustrated wall map of the world. The circular bar itself was originally crafted from the timbers of a Spanish Galleon, wound with heavy sailing rope and is adorned with footrests and handholds of ornately carved whales' teeth. It features a glass top over a lighted relief of the sea, which depicts the development of ships throughout history with tiny model ships that can be moved around by magnets. The famous barstools are still covered in whale foreskin, a fact that Onassis loved to tell his guests, especially the women. The barstools were an exotic, sexually charged touch thoroughly enjoyed by Onassis.

The Lapis Lounge owes its name to the breathtaking lapis lazuli fireplace, which is the focal point of the room that was a favorite place for Richard Burton and Elizabeth Taylor to relax and enjoy while they were on board the ship. Bookshelves surrounding the fireplace are filled with rare volumes. There are fine pieces of art including a Renoir, Le Corbusier and de Chirico, which adorn the walls. It is the perfect place to unwind and savor the beauty of this magnificent ship.

The swimming pool/dance floor were carefully restored by an apprentice of the original craftsmen, the floor of the bronze-bordered swimming pool is inlaid with an exquisite mosaic copied directly from the Palace of Knossos in Crete. With a push of a button, the bottom of the pool rises above the water to become a dance floor just as it did in the days of Onassis. It is everyone's fantasy to dance under the stars with the moon looking down creating a romantic mood. It is so easy to enjoy oneself just as Onassis and his guests did when they partied on board.

The atrium is highlighted by a majestic spiral staircase with an onyx and silver handrail, which circles and connects the three cabin decks. A delicate mural winds up the surrounding wall and a central mosaic with the Christina Yachting emblem adorns the floor. It is a most impressive and imposing entryway and leaves most guests awestruck by the artistic aura.

The Spa Complex encompasses half the Promenade Deck, including a fitness, center, massage room, sports lounge and beauty salon. The sumptuous Jacuzzi Deck is fitted with a Jacuzzi, and open air bar and al fresco dining. This is the perfect place for guests to unwind and relax and enjoy while they holiday at sea.

The Main Dining Room can easily accommodate up to 40 guests and features fine hand-finished tables, Venetian lace tablecloths, Waterford glassware, Ercuis silver ware and a sunken marble floor. What a fabulous place to dine and delight in visiting with the other guests aboard the Christina O! The creative cuisine served takes on new dimensions while dining at sea.

When one desires a quiet moment to reflect and relax, the Library is filled with books from around the world. They are published in several languages providing guests with a variety of works. It is a special place to read some rare volumes or to work at one of the two writing desks. It is an ideal location to record ones thoughts and memories of this voyage to enjoy at a later time.

The Music Lounge features a grand piano, Italian furniture by Giorgetti. There is a large collection of Maria Callas's memorabilia to enjoy including her sole gold record. One can just imagine her standing there by the piano singing to the guests on board with Onassis proudly looking on.

The Show Lounge is equipped with a presentation platform and Giorgetti furniture. The enormous bay windows offer panoramic views of the ocean. This lounge houses video equipment and a stereo system for their passengers' enjoyment. It is here that the stars of the silver screen compete with the stars overlooking the sea and the enchanted evenings aboard.

The Children's Playroom is brightly decorated and provides a perfect spot for children to get together with a large selection of toys for their amusement. Many a wonderful afternoon is spent here with children of all ages having a fabulous time.

The Tenders and Water Sports Equipment are comprised of two-twelve passenger Hacker Craft mahogany tenders, water-ski boat, two jet skis, wind surfers and snorkeling gear. There is everything imaginable for water enjoyment while on the ship and in port. Every swimmers fantasy is possible in this opulent setting.

Now, after more than a quarter-century, the yacht returns to sail into the new millennium in all of her original grandeur complemented by today's latest technology. As the Christina O yacht begins a new era in history, it offers individuals the opportunity to book passage and become a part of her illustrious legacy, an option never before available on a private luxury mega-yacht.

Champagne and caviar awaits you when you book passage on the Christina O! Eight days are spent exploring both well known and lesser known Greek islands. It is a rare opportunity sail along the seas made famous by many famous explorers from Greek mythology. Evenings are enjoyed aboard the legendary yacht with international cuisine accompanied by celebrated wines. No detail is overlooked in the crews' quest to make this the most memorable voyage of one's lifetime.

In the true Onassis fashion, a cruise on the Christina 0 is the opportunity to experience not only the finer things in life but it is the ultimate life experience. You become a part of the history of this ship, the same history shared by all those who preceded you on this gracious, opulent vessel. This journey back into time will touch your soul as you visit antiquity while residing on the original ship of the first Jet Setters. It is the perfect blending of the old and the new, the then and now.

We can only imagine what secrets the Christina holds in the bosom of her hull. When all is said and done, the Onassis Odyssey was without doubt a tale that was as exciting and inspiring as any other tale from Greek mythology.

About The Author:

Who is January Jones?

She is NOT a young, beautiful actress on Mad Men!

She is NOT an older, gorgeous exotic dancer *from the*

Johnny Carson Show!

She is an AUTHOR...........*Thou Shalt Not Whine...The Eleventh Commandment, Jackie Ari & Jack: The Tragic Love Triangle, Oh, No....Jackie-O! & Priceless Personalities: Volume 1 and The Christina: The Onassis Odyssey.*

She is a TALK SHOW HOST ...... with ITV at Talk4Radio with a Strategic Media Partnership at iHeartRadio Talk with over 30 million listeners and BlogTalkRadio.com with over 1.8 million listeners.

She is a Kennedy Expert...3 books & over 500 interviews

She is a REALITY TV GOLF PERSONALITY...... World High Stakes Golf televised on HD Net

She is a RADIO & TV GUEST PERSONALITY....500 radio talk show interviews

She is a Cruise Ship Speaker..... Norwegian Cruise Line.

She is a HUMORIST & WHINE-OLOGIST.... Member

Association of Applied Therapeutic Humor (AATH)

More About The Author:

Ms. January Jones is the author of ***Thou Shalt Not Whine....The Eleventh Commandment*** published by Beaufort Books. Her book is based on a survey of the top ten things that people whine about and reached #1 at amazon.com.

Ms. Jones has written 3 books about Jackie Kennedy: ***Oh, No....Jackie-O!, Jackie Ari & Jack:The Tragic Love Triangle*** *and now* ***The Christina: The Onassis Odyssey: Celebrities, Courtship and Chaos.***

Ms. Jones hosts, "January Jones sharing Success Stories" on The Intertainment Network/W4CY and iHeart Radio Talk with 30 million listeners and January is a "Featured Host" at BlogTalkRadio.com with over 1.8 million listeners to date.

January is a speaker, talk radio personality, cruise ship speaker, a reality TV golfer and a humorist in the tradition of Erma Bombeck. Ms. Jones has done over 500 radio and TV interviews promoting her theories with humor and hope.

Ms. Jones was the owner-manager of The Thousand Oaks Racquet Club in thousand, Oaks, CA for 20 years. She attended the University of Detroit and is a recipient of The Irwin Award and the RTIR Quantum Leap Award. She is an honorary Naval Aviator on U. S. S. Carl Vinson and the recipient of the Earl Warren Medal from the United States Government.

Website: http://www.januaryjones.com/

CONTACT: info@januaryjones.com LinkedIn, Twitter, Facebook, YouTube: iJanuaryJones Channel

Bibliography

Adams, Cindy and Crimp, Susan. Iron Rose: The Story of Rose Fitzgerald Kennedy and Her Dynasty. Beverly Hills, CA: Dove Books, 1995.

Adler, Bill. The Last Will and Testament of Jacqueline Kennedy Onassis. New York: Carroll and Graf Publishers, 1997.

Adler, Bill. The Uncommon Wisdom of Jacqueline Kennedy. New York: A Citadel Press Book published by Carol Publishing Co., 1994

Andersen, Christopher. Jackie After Jack. New York: William Morrow and Company, Inc.,1998.

Andersen, Christopher. Jack and Jackie: Portrait of an American Marriage. New York: William Morrow and Company Inc., 1996

Anthony, Carl Serfrazza. As We Remember Her. New York: Harper Collins, 1997

Belzer, Richard. UFOs, JFK, and Elvis. New York: Ballantine Books, 1999.

Bly, Nellie. The Kennedy Men: Three Generations of Sex, Scandal and Secrets. New York: Kensington Publishing Corp., 1996

Bradlee, Ben. A Good Life. New York: Simon and Schuster, 1995.

Brown, Joanne. Passion Gate. Washington, D.C.: The NF Journal Press, 1997.

Cafarkis, Christian. The Fabulous Onassis: His Life and Loves. New York: William Morrow and Co. me., 1972.

Carroll, Gerald A. Project Seek: Onassis, Kennedy and the Gemstone Theory. Carson City, NV: Bridger House Publishers, 1994.

Collier, Peter and Horowitz, David. The Kennedys: An American Drama. New York: Wamer Books, 1984.

Condon, Dianne RusselL Jackie's Treasures. New York: Clarkson Potter Publishers, 1996.

David, Lester. Jacqueline Kennedy Onassis. New York: A Brich Lane Press Book, 1994.

Davis, John H. Jacqueline Bouvier: An Intimate Memoir. New York: John Wiley and Sons, me., 1996.

Davis, John H. The Kennedys: Dynasty and Disaster 1848-1983. New York: John Wiley and Sons, me., 1984.

Davis, L.J. Onassis, Aristotle and Christina. New York: St. Martin's Press, 1986.

Davis, Lee. Assassination, Twenty Assassinations That Changed History. New York: BDD Special Editions, 1993.

Du Bois, Diana. In Her Sister's Shadow. Boston: Little, Brown and Co., 1995.

Evans, Peter. Ari: The Life and Times of Aristotle Onassis. New York: Summit Books, 1986.

Fraser, Nicolas, Jacobson, Philip, Ottaway, Mark, Chester, Lewis. Aristotle Onassis. Philadelphia & New York:

Lippincott Co., 1977.

Gentry, Curt. J. Edgar Hoover: The Man and The Secrets. New York: W.W. Norton and Co., 1991.

Goodwin, Doris Kearns. The Fitzgeralds and The Kennedys: An American Saga. New York: St. Martin's Press, 1987.

Hamilton, Nigel. JFK Reckless Youth. New York: Random House, 1992,

Hersh, Seymour M. The Dark Side of Camelot. Boston: Little, Brown and Co., 1997.

Heymann, C. David. A Woman Named Jackie. New York: A Lyle Stuart Book, 1989.

Hurt, Henry. The Assassination of John F. Kennedy. New York: Holt, Rinehart and Winston, 1985.

Keith, Jim. The Gemstone File. Avondale, GA: lllumiNet Press, 1992.

Kelley, Kitty. Jackie Oh! New York: Ballantine Books, 1979.

Klein, Edward. All Too Human: The Love Story of Jack and Jackie Kennedy. New York: Pocket Books, 1996.

Klein, Edward. Just Jackie: Her Private Years. New York: Ballantine Books, 1998.

Leamer, Laurence. The Kennedy Women. New York: Villard Books, 1994.

Martin, Ralph. A Hero For Our Times. New York: Fawcett Crest, 1983.

Martin, Ralph. Seeds of Destruction. New York: G. P. Putman's Sons, 1995.

Osborne, Claire G. Jackie: A Legend Defined. New York: Avon Books, 1997.

Reeves, Richard. President Kennedy: Profile of Power. New York: Simon and Schuster, 1993.

Reeves, Richard. A Question of Character. Rocklin, CA: Prima Publishing, 1992.

Scott, Michael. Maria Meneghini Callas. Boston: Northeastern University Press, 1992.

Sloan, Bill. JFK Breaking The Silence. Dallas: Taylor Publishing Co., 1993.

Stone, Oliver. JFK: The Book of The Film. New York: Applause Books, 1992.

Strober, Deborah and Gerald S. "Let Us Begin Anew": An Oral History of The Kennedy Presidency. New York: Harper Collins, 1993.

Printed in Great Britain
by Amazon